HAVING EARLY VISIONS THAT MOVE MOUNTAINS
MY WINNING PURPOSE

ERIC S. YORK

LifeRich Publishing is a registered trademark of The Reader's Digest Association, Inc.

LifeRich Publishing books may be ordered through booksellers or by contacting:

LifeRich Publishing
1663 Liberty Drive
Bloomington, IN 47403
www.liferichpublishing.com
844-686-9607

Because of the dynamic nature of the Internet, any web addresses or links contained in this book may have changed since publication and may no longer be valid. The views expressed in this work are solely those of the author and do not necessarily reflect the views of the publisher, and the publisher hereby disclaims any responsibility for them.

Any people depicted in stock imagery provided by Getty Images are models, and such images are being used for illustrative purposes only.
Certain stock imagery © Getty Images.

Scripture taken from the New King James Version®. Copyright © 1982 by Thomas Nelson. Used by permission. All rights reserved.

ISBN: 978-1-4897-1771-9 (sc)
ISBN: 978-1-4897-1774-0 (e)

Print information available on the last page.

LifeRich Publishing rev. date: 08/24/2021

Special Dedication

**I dedicate this Hall of Fame Edition to the memory of grandmother Idella Green. I will always love you and miss you.
Rest in Peace**

DOES GOD HAVE A VISION FOR YOU?

God has made everyone with many things in common. However, each person is well-defined made not like any other human being.

God has a great plan, a *vision* which includes you. It's the reason you are here. You are special and different from anyone else. The great Creator God personally designed and made you that way. Therefore, you have a **contribution (impact) offer** that no one else can make.

The difference between a chump and a champion is *commitment, enthusiasm,* and *commitment* demand *purpose, faith* and *vision-daily vision.*

Visionaries having a *vision* are able to *visualize.* *Visualizing* is the beginning of a completed *vision.*

CHAPTER 1

EMBRACING THE RACE OF LIFE

I was born in Quincy, Florida which is a small and historic city. The first house which I grew up in was a wood house that had a tin roof with no running water. The house was located out in the country behind a large corn field about ten miles from the Florida and Georgia state line. My father Bennie L. York, Jr., mother Jacqueline V. York, and grandmother Idella Green drove about four miles to the fresh crystal-clear water spring. The fresh crystal-clear water spring flowed out the end of the long line pipes was located beside the road and above halfway of the deep ditch. A big pond was located nearby across from the deep ditch through the forests. The family walked down in the ditch to bring up spring water in gallon jugs. This was the best spring water that I had ever tasted in my life. The spring water was cool and fresh with an enjoyable taste. Buckets of water were used

1

in the kitchen for washing dishes. The family also put buckets all the way through the house to catch the water from the ceiling while it rained. A metal tub was used for taken bathes. Father, mother, and grandmother took the dirty clothes to the laundry mat in town to be washed and dried.

The outhouse was made out of wood and had a tin roof. There were no running water or electric lights inside of the bathroom. The bathroom was located separately beside the house on the front left side. I could remember going to the outhouse in the summer and winter months during the mornings, days, and nights. We used sometimes moss from the trees and sears catalogs as bathroom tissue. The maggot worms would be going around in the toilet with squeaky sounds as you were using it.

The house had only a front door and back door. The front door was the only door locked during the night. The front door had a gate latch lock with a key that was used to open the door. A wood board was placed on the front door for extra security at night time. The living room with a table and the dining room were used as one room. The living room also had a steel heater that burned wood in the earlier years but was later replaced with a gas heater. There were only two bed rooms in the house. The rooms didn't have doors but included plastic curtains used as doors. The rooms got cold a lot of times. Kerosene heaters were used in the rooms for heat. The windows were opened to bring fresh air into the house and to cool it off. There were electric lights in every room inside of the house. The electric irons were used for ironing clothes. The gas stove was in the kitchen. The gas tank was on the side of the house. Father had hogs in a hog pen outside in the field. I was four years old when my family moved out from the country to the city.

We moved into a new yellow and red brick house. The house had black shingles on the roof and a small tree in the middle of the front yard. The house was located on Experiment Station Road. There was a short cement drive way from the highway and stopped in front of the living room. The new house had two main entrances which were a front and a back door. Both of the doors had doorknobs that were locked with keys. Many times, during the nights we pulled out a top drawer in front of the back door for safety reasons. The new house had a living room, kitchen, hallway, three bedrooms, one bathroom, one laundry room, and an outside utility room on the back left side of the house. Tile floors were in the living room, kitchen, and the laundry room. All of the bed rooms and the hallway had carpet on the floors. The outside utility room's floor was made out of cement.

The house had utilities such as electricity, water, and gas. The air conditioner unit was in a window between the living room and the kitchen. The air conditioner blew the air down the hallway and throughout the house. The ceiling fans in the rooms helped to circulate the air. The windows were opened to bring fresh air into the house and to cool it off. A gas stove was in the kitchen. The gas tank was behind the house between the back door and the outside utility room.

Mother bought a few five-gallon fish aquariums, and some ten-gallon fish aquariums, and tropical fish for the living room. I bought gold fish and fish bowls, and one blue and red tropical fish in its own bowl with water for the bedroom of brother and I throughout the years.

A clothesline made with six wood poles a total of three rows with wires from pole to pole for drying clothes were in the middle of the back yard. We used clothespins to attach the clothes to the clotheslines. The dog house was located behind the left side of the clothesline. Later, during the years a fence was placed around the dog house. The dog house with a fence around it was called a dog pin. We owned different types of dog breeds throughout the years. We owned these types of dogs a black and brown beagle, black Labrador retriever, black and white bull dog mix, golden chow, and two German shepherds. Brother Felix A. York, Sr. and I built a tree house each year for three years. The Chinaberry Tree located behind the right side on the clothesline on the edge of the yard. Brother placed electric doorbells in two of the tree houses. The basketball goal was located to the right side of the Chinaberry Tree in the back corner of the yard.

The beginning of my early childhood years, my grandfather Bennie L. York, Sr. of Edison, Georgia would have me sit on his lap most of the time. Grandfather would come to visit and play with me. I laughed most of the time while I was sitting on his lap. He was like a great, big, gentle, and black teddy bear. Grandfather was a great baseball player, but he was very big with those red eyes. Grandfather would hit home runs most of the time, so he could walk around the bases. I was four years old when my grandfather passed away.

I was taken by my mother to the first day of school at Stewart Street Elementary. Mother walked me and dropped me off to Ms. Dillard and her class.

They were standing in a straight line outside of the elementary building. I started to miss mother as she walked towards her car in the back main parking lot. Mother had walked almost to her car. I cried as I left the class and ran towards mother. Mother said, "She looked back and saw me running up the hill with my little red bag." Mother turned around and took me back to Ms. Dillard who was still standing outside with the class.

One afternoon while Ms. Dillard gave out snacks, she told the class not to talk during nap time. However, after nap time had started, one of my girl classmates and I decided to talk as we laid on the floor beside each other. Ms. Dillard called my classmate and I to her desk. Ms. Dillard said, "You all shouldn't be talking during nap time. I'm going give both of you a whipping." After my classmate and I received our whippings, we walked back to our nap time spots and went to sleep.

I was placed in a speech class during my fourth and fifth grades. I had a stuttering problem when I spoke words. Mrs. Carolyn L. Bridges-Smith was a great speech teacher and my speaking skills had gotten incredibly better at the end of my fourth-grade year.

I was eight years old when I stood in the backyard in Quincy, Florida as the sun setting and going down.

I asked God what to do with my life. The *visions* that God gave me were to earn a college degree and to be a great football player. I just wanted a chance to accomplish both of those *dreams*.

I sat on the sofa while watching football games on television. I had *dreams* of playing professional football. *I also asked God to help me to be the best person that I could become in life. I knew it would take a lot of putting God first, focus, dedication, and sacrifice with hard work to become the best.* I was willing to do whatever it took to accomplish my goals in an honest and respectable **purpose driven path**.

Purpose **is the reason for using our own gifts, talents, skills, and experience with determination**

to serve God by loving people and making this world a better place. A <u>goal</u> has one or more objectives to be achieved which are observable and measurable for wanted results within a time period. It was important for me to accomplish my goals without cheating and cutting corners.

> "Humbleness, effort, hard work, accountability, and being a servant is the recipe for excellence, everyone will not achieve greatness."
>
> **Eric S. York**

My father, mother, and grandmother encouraged having faith by attending Mt. Hosea Missionary Baptist Church on a regular basis. It is important to have a strong foundational support system which produces the **anchor** for life.

After a Sunday morning church service at 11 am, the people were walking out of the church. I was walking at the beginning of the center aisle towards the back double doors. A middle-aged man approached me as I walked down the narrow walkway. The deacon said, "If you have more good days than bad days, you have lived a good life."

The next Sunday morning service during offering time, two deacons were standing behind a table in front of the altar. Before people started to walk in front of the table, the deacon standing on the right side called people up to the table to help collect money. The deacon who talked to me the week before was asking people to come up to the table to help with collecting money. I was sitting on a middle pew at the left side of the church. I was one of the two people that the deacon chose to help collect the offerings. The deacon standing on the left side prayed over the money after all of it was placed on the table. Two weeks later, the deacon died who asked me to help with collecting the money.

My grandmother noticed I was going to be great one day. Grandmother, brother, and I walked sometimes from her apartment about three miles to the Winn-Dixie grocery store. One day, grandmother looked up at the Store Manager Mr. Jim Miller who was standing in the upper office area. Grandmother pointing down at me and said, "This is a special child who is going to be great one day."

Grandmother also took my brother and I to a lady in her apartment complex who sold candy. A few months before grandmother passed away, she took us to get some candy. Grandmother told the lady to let my boys get whatever they want to purchase. Grandmother had never told the lady to do this before. Grandmother was very sick, and said to my mother about a year before I got my diploma, "I think I'm not going to see Eric graduate from high school." Grandmother died in January, and I graduated from high school on June seventh of nineteen eighty-eight.

Grandmothers Idella Green, Alice Grace-York, Marjorie Robinson, and Aunt Dorothy A. Hamilton-Reese passed down love and life lessons to our family. We spent a large amount of time at their homes. We also spent some time at the uncles, aunts, and cousins' houses. We had great family gatherings of fellowship and food throughout the years. The Thanksgiving and Christmas holidays were precious and cherished times for our family. *I was taught the **right and wrong choices** at an early age which helped me with **making good decisions in life**.* **God gave man the Free Will to make choices and decisions.** *Choices* **are actions of making decisions when challenged with two or more possibilities.** *Decisions* **are processes for choosing somethings or answering questions.** Once, I had accepted the *visions* that God gave me, the love, guidance, and correctional measures empowered me to make better life choices and not give up. I was strengthened by *good life values* to be able to overcome mistakes and obstacles that I would meet in my life.

I'm from a middle-class family who didn't have a lot of money. However, my brother Felix A. York, Sr., sister Jocelin L. York, and I didn't go without shelter, food, or clothes. Father and mother graduated from high school but didn't attend college. My father was a great baseball and football player in high school.

I grew up during the soulful and exciting years of the seventies and eighties. These were the years of the afros' hair styles, bell bottom pants, 8-track tapes for playing music, many people would put aluminum foil on their television antennas, and sometimes used metal clothes' hangers as television antennas. It was black and white along with color televisions in homes and businesses. Most of the time in those years, the television stations went off the air at night between twelve and two o'clock in the morning with the playing of "The Star-Spangled Banner." It was no cable and satellite television during this time.

Uncle Curtis "Walking Curtis" Grace-York came to our house one special Friday night. Uncle Curtis wore a white t-shirt, black dress pants, black belt, white tube socks, and black dress shoes. Mother turned the television off as soon as the news went off at 11:30 pm and then turned on our floor model stereo 8-track tape player. Uncle Curtis started dancing wildly with his fancy turns while putting black lines of scuff marks all over the white tile floor. Mother told my brother and I about 1 am that you all will have to get those black scuff marks off of the floor in the morning. Uncle Curtis danced until 2:30 am in the morning, and then he went home. Early Saturday morning about 8 am brother and I got two tooth brushes and filled two buckets up with water. We put baking soda on our tooth brushes and dipped them in the buckets. We got down on our knees. It took brother and I several hours to get the black lines of scuff marks off of the floor.

Mother took my ten years old brother and I who was eleven years old to see the movie Purple Rain at the dollar movie in Tallahassee, Florida. This movie was one of Prince's best classics.

The boys and girls passed sometimes love letters on a piece of paper across the classroom to each other. The love letters would say to check or circle either yes or no if you like me.

The children played with fireworks such as snaps, sparklers, firecrackers, jumping jacks, roman candles, rockets, bottle rockets, skyrockets, and *fountains* during the nights close to and on New Year's Day, Memorial Day, and the Forth of July.

Mother regularly told brother and I after school to do our homework, house chores, and change into our play clothes before we went outside to play. The children of our neighborhood were very talented at playing sports, so we spent a large amount of time playing outside in the yards, on the streets, and at the Bobby Nealy Sports Complex. The Bobby Nealy Sports Complex was about a half of a mile walk or drive from my house. Men and women played in recreation leagues of softball and flag football at this park. The children went from yard to yard, street to street, and every so often traveled to other neighborhoods to play with each other. We spent a lot of time outside playing with marbles, kickball, football, softball, basketball, horseshoes, flew kites, and baseball replaced sometimes with a tennis ball. We also played freeze tag, hide and go seek, red light-green light, four square, hopscotch, and tug of war.

The children played occasionally with different types of video games inside of their houses, Pizza Hut, video arcade stores, and at other places. The Atari and Nintendo were the most popular video game systems at this time. Atari has awesome video games such as Pac-Man, Ms. Pac-Man, Defender, Centipede, Asteroids, Battlezone, Missile Command, and Space Invaders. Nintendo has great video games such as Donkey Kong, Metroid, Pokémon, and Super Mario.

The children also played with electronic handheld games of the seventies and eighties.

The children played sometimes with Rubik's Cubes, playing cards, and board games inside and outside of their houses. The children played with uno cards and the playing cards included games of spades, bid whist, gold fish, and I declare war. We played board games such as Checkers, Chess, Operation, Monopoly, and Candy Land. The children also rode their tricycles, bicycles, and go carts in the yards, on the roads and streets. We opened our gifts on Christmas Eve and Christmas Day. The season of Christmas is my favorite time of the year. The moments were priceless as we opened and enjoyed our presents.

The parents and the older children taught the younger children *life values* and how to play correctly. The parents and the older children participated sometimes and gave love, wisdom, and toughness to the younger children.

The children played regularly in the neighbors' yards and got into trouble sometimes by doing something wrong. The neighbor talked to you or also gave you a whipping. The neighbor often called your parents before you got home. Once you got home, your parent or parents talked to you or also gave you a whipping. Additionally, the neighbors borrowed every so often cups of sugar, flour, rice, grits, beans, eggs, and other things from each other. Many of the neighbors were family or acted like family members to each other.

The children went to Buster Smart's Food and Grocery Store to buy snacks. A lady sold Dixie cups made of frozen Kool-Aid in paper cups at her home. The Dixie cups were great cold treats for the hot summer days.

The *gnats* (insects) known as nats were awfully bad from mid-July to August were called dog days. Mother told my younger brother and I to be home before the street lights came on. We played outside from sunrise to sunset many times for years during the summer months.

My brother was ten years old and I was eleven years old when our baby sister was born. Mother took brother, sister, and I regularly to spend time with our grandmothers. We also stayed sometimes overnight throughout the weekends at our grandmothers' houses. *We got a lot of love, life principles, and good food from our grandmothers.* The grandmothers taught us a great amount of wisdom from the days when they were growing up.

Father spent most of his time working and after

work was frequently busy. However, father took my brother and I to his baseball and softball games. We also went fishing and hunting with my father, uncles, cousins, and friends. Father also found time to take our friend Joseph Washington III who lived next door, my brother, and I to our little league football and baseball practices as well as the games. The coaches always said, "I was either the second or third best player on my little league teams." Joseph and I went to a football practice at Carter Paramore Middle School. The team was made up of eighth and nineth graders. The nineth graders were very big, so Joseph and I decided to play our last year of little league football. We had wanted to go back and try to win a little league championship for Head Coach Bobby Nealy and Southern Electric. After being very close for years of not beating the top team, we finally won the little league football championship!

CHAPTER 2

FOLLOW YOUR DREAMS

I did a lot of training by running in the hot sun in the summer months preparing for my ninth-grade year football camp in August 1984 at Carter Paramore Middle School. The heat felt like an air conditioner unit to me because I had run a lot in the sun which helped me greatly throughout camp to not get tired and dehydrated. I was the third best player on the depth chart at the strong safety position in the beginning of the football camp. I didn't play the first two games of the season. I had two bigger players who got a chance to start and play before me. However, I was the starter of the third game of the season and played the rest of the year. **Let's go Lions!**

The beginning of my tenth-grade year at James A. High School, I was a hard worker who spent most of summer in the weight room and running before football season. Players, coaches, and sometimes guys from the community were in the weight room. I was one of the smallest players in the weight room with the biggest heart. Woodrow Hinson and another guy who had graduated and played football at the high school; mentored and trained me in the weight room. Woodrow and the guy saw my determination to be the best. We were sometimes the only three people left in the weight room. The weight room didn't have an air conditioner or a heating unit during this time. The weight room was located across the street from the high school in a city building. The city building has in it a storage room, weight room, and locker room. The city building was located on the corner of N. Graves Street and W. King Street, in front of Corey Field, and beside the baseball field. Joe Ferolito Recreation Center was located directly across the street from the baseball field.

The start of the summer football camp in August 1985, I had participated in a tackling drill on the baseball field's outfield. It was two lines with one line made up of the players who ran the football. I was in the line of the players who ran the football and stood in the back of the line. I jumped in front of the line when I saw a fellow upcoming tenth grader in front of the line of the tacklers. The coach blew the whistle. I took about three steps, and my teammate hit me head up. The two lines of players were about thirty yards away from each other. I was running high and didn't get a chance to protect myself, so we ran and hit each other with the front of our helmets. I had an old helmet with a hard forehead pad with three splits in the middle of it. I left the baseball field where the defense had just finished with practice. I walked towards the locker room. An offensive player was leaving the football field. The football field was located beside the baseball field. I was about to go into the locker room when the offensive player approached me. The player said, "York, you have a huge bump on your forehead." I said, "ok" as I went into the locker room and got dressed. I got on my bicycle and rode to the store to get a drink. The store was located across the road from the baseball field. Afterwards, I got on my bicycle and rode home about five miles. Once I got home, I went to the bathroom and looked in the mirror at my face. I saw a huge bump on my forehead. I went to the kitchen, got a zip lock bag, and put ice in it to place on my forehead. I spent several hours putting the bag of ice on my forehead and going back to the mirror to look at it but the injury still left a good size bump.

I had a good season at the beginning and until the fourth game of the year as a backup outside linebacker and a special teams' player. The fourth game of the season was the homecoming celebration week. The stadium was filled with fans and standing room only on homecoming night at Corey Field. The freshness of the crisp winter air also made it great for Friday night football.

A neighboring high school football team, the Taylor County Bulldogs from Perry, Florida was ranked number three in the state of Florida. We were not achieving a lot of wins during those years. The senior outside linebacker who started in front of me was struggling with making plays most of the first half. One of the defensive coaches took the senior linebacker out of the game a little before the end of the second quarter. The coach placed me into the game.

After the senior linebacker went to the sideline, he threw his helmet against the fence and then kicked the fence. The beginning of the third quarter, I ran from far across the field from the end of the line of scrimmage to sack the quarterback on the sideline. The hit caused the quarterback to go one way and the football to go the other way. We recovered the fumble and went in to score a touchdown. Our next defensive series of plays for the third quarter, I was rushing again from the right end of the defensive line. I blocked the punt which seemed to roll for thirty yards before anyone could hold onto the football. The fifth player went after the football was able to recover it for us. The next series of offensive plays, we went in to score another touchdown. We came back to win the game.

Everyone was very happy and excited because we had won especially on homecoming night. After the game, our team was in the locker room. Robert Harris was the starting senior tailback with tears in his eyes and standing by the cake table. Robert told the lady who was cutting the cake to gave me his piece of homecoming cake. I was standing next to Robert by the cake table. Robert said, "You really gave the quarterback a hard hit." He was very happy for the win on his last homecoming game. I started the rest of the season as one of the two outside linebackers.

I began to mentally and physically prepare like a college football player at the start of the summer of my junior year. I did a ten-mile run in the hot sun from my house along the side of the roads to the other side of town and returned back at the house. I also ran up, down hills, and back paddle up them to increase my explosiveness and cardiovascular system. The powerful workouts on the hills gave me great speed, power, and endurance to last longer. My brother and I went to the weight room on a regular basis.

I started at outside linebacker until the fourth game of the season. The fourth game was the middle of the football season. I was having a good season. The team was practicing after school on a Tuesday afternoon getting ready for the fifth game of the season. The linebackers were participating in a tackling drill. The drill was made up of two lines; one line for the ball carriers and the other line for the tacklers. The lines were about fifteen yards away from each other. I was running the football when a teammate's helmet hit me in the middle of my right front thigh to give me a deep thigh bruise. It took a month and a half for my thigh to heal, so I didn't play anymore during the season.

I decided to try out for the track and field team in the second semester of my junior year to increase my speed for football. We had a great track team with Coach James W. Pelham who mentored like a father gave us love, confidence, and a good work ethic. The practices took place most of the time on the track field at the school. The track field was made of broken pieces of hard asphalt rocks, dirt, and sand. We were taught good track and field techniques by the use of drills which produced good competition between us. The long side walk beside the highway, a few feet across from the apartments, a few feet away on the other side of the track field, and straight down the road from the high school provided a great path to run up and down hills. We had to run up and down the long side walk without stopping until completing the total number for the workout.

We were given a three-mile run. The path of the run started at the high school to the Mining Factory in the country and then back to the high school. Coach Pelham rode up and down the road in his car. If you stopped at any time in the path of the run, coach stopped, picked you up, and took you back to the school, and you have to start over. Some of my teammates stopped running and were taken back to start over. I was never taken back to the school to start over because I didn't stop running. I ran at a steady pace most of the time. *My determination taught me the lesson to not to give up when times get tough in life.*

I trained very hard in the summer months preparing for my senior season. I trained in the weight room almost every day and sometimes by myself. I jogged on the roads during the hot afternoons. I also ran hills in the cool mornings and throughout the hot afternoons. I always took it easy from training the week before camp because you need to be mentally and physically refreshed before practice. I drove up town to the Allen Sports store. I bought an orange pair of orange wrist bands and shoe strings to reward myself for training very hard during the summer. I had planned to treasure my last year of playing high school football.

The middle of the football camp in August 1987 after daily practices, I got a rash on my chest and back from the wet shoulder pads. The rash arrived on my body because of the sweat, and the pads not getting a chance to dry completely. Mother took me up town to the Massey Drugs store. The old man who worked in the pharmacy told my mother that I needed to put dandruff shampoo on my chest and back before going to bed each night. Today, I still have the rash that comes back sometimes.

I had a good senior year as an outside linebacker most of the season. I was honored in The Gadsden County Times newspaper as a member of the All County and Big Bend Team. **Let's go Tigers!**

I took the ACT college entrance test four times but couldn't pass it the second semester of my senior year. I took the test two times after Friday night football games on Saturdays' mornings. I was still very tired after playing the football games. I also took the test two more times after the season. I made a lower score each time I took the test and didn't pass it. It is important to start preparing and taking the college entrance tests at least by your tenth-grade year. *You should not wait until the twelve-grade year to prepare and take the college entrance test.* I graduated from high school with a 2.9 grade point average. *I should have passed the college entrance test before my senior year and used better study habits.* The preparatory classes, the study guides, and tutoring are *valuable tools* for passing the test. Mother regularly said, "Eric just don't look at the pictures in the sports' section but read the newspaper sometimes."

I was on the weight lifting team in the second semester of my junior and senior years. My height was 6'1, weighed 176 pounds, and bench pressed 295 pounds on the weight lifting team at the end of the second semester of my senior year. My goal was to bench press over 300 pounds before I graduated from high school. However, my last asthma attack which I felt like a fish with no water and was about to die caused me not to bench press over 300 pounds.

The only college football letters that I received was from my Head Coach Alexander James almost every day of the second semester came from a division III school. The school didn't offer scholarships. The school was located up north, so I knew paying for it and traveling would both be a problem. I decided not to go to the school. The first letter stated the coaches have noticed you making many great defensive plays on film while we were scouting a player on the other team.

Some of my teammates were being recruited and playing football at Tuskegee University. I had grown up with these players. An assistant coach of our football team had played at Tuskegee University was suggesting players to the coaching staff at the University. I had really wanted to go to college with my neighborhood friends. I called the coach one afternoon and asked him will you help me to attend Tuskegee University to play football? The coach said, "no" to my *dream* of becoming a golden tiger football player.

One day after practice about the end of my senior track season, I stood beside and talked to Coach Pelham. I told Coach Pelham I wanted to play college football. Coach Pelham said, "You will not be able to play the same position in college because of your size." The *advice* encouraged me to become even more determined to be a great college football player. I knew because of my purpose. I had to become bigger, stronger, and faster to be one of the best.

CHAPTER 4

THE JOURNEY BEGINS

The history of my ancestors the slaves were the first motivation that encouraged me to go to college. A slave is owned by another person. A human being classified as property and who is made to work for nothing. Individuals are owned by others who control where they live and the kind of work. Slavery had earlier lasted during the course of history in many times and most places. All of the ancient Greeks, Romans, Incas, and Aztecs were slave owners.

Slavery was started when a Portuguese slave ship went across the Atlantic Ocean with a lower room department filled with imprisoned Africans from Angola in southwestern Africa. The first locked up Africans arrived in Jamestown for slavery on August 20, 1619. Angolans were captured by the Portuguese and arrived in the British colony of Virginia to be bought by English colonists.

The slaves were sold up to four times what the buyers had paid for them. People paid $1,200 for a slave which is equal to almost $30,000.

The slave owners used some house slaves who performed chores such as raised the slave owners' children, cleaned, cooked, served food and drinks. Some of the slaves worked outside did landscaping in the yard. The slaves worked as carpenters, coopers, boatmen, cooks, seamstresses, and blacksmiths are only a few of the skilled duties required around plantations. Many slaves were involved in the building of roads. However, most of the slaves' labor were used in planting, cultivating, and harvesting cotton, hemp, rice, tobacco, or sugar cane. The slaves weren't paid money. The master regularly decided how a slave was treated by his or her skill level and value. The slaves only received the clothes on their bodies and a place to live.

The process of slavery was about money, power, and control. Slavery developed a lot of racism and hatred towards people. Many slaves didn't get a chance to read and write because they weren't allowed to go to school. The slaves sneaked books to read and secretly organized private school settings.

Christianity had spread through the slave community just before the beginning of the Civil

War. All of the slaves weren't Christians nor were all those who agreed to be Christian members of a church. However, most of the slaves were aware of the doctrines, symbols, and *vision* of life preached by Christianity. The religion of the slaves was both visible and invisible, formally organized, and spur-of-the-moment changed. Regular Sunday worship in the local church was duplicated by unlawful or at least casual, prayer meetings on weeknights in the slave cabins. Preachers licensed by the church and hired by the master were paid only by the spirit. The preachers didn't receive a payment of money for their service. Passages from the Bible which most slaves could not read were explained by verses from holy songs. Slaves prevented by masters to go to church or in some cases, even to pray, risked beatings to attend secret gatherings to worship God. The secret gatherings of worship by the slaves were known as invisible churches.

The slave owners were afraid if the slaves learned to read, they will gain knowledge and understanding from the messages. The slaves may become disobedient and try to escape. Slaves who tried to escape were often chased and captured by their slave owners, hired slave hunters, law enforcement officers, and dogs. The slaves who disobeyed their owners or the slave laws were punished in terrible ways such as got beating on their backs with whips, tree hangings, and other life-threatening punishment measures. Hundreds of slaves escaped to the North and became free slaves. Famous slaves who made an impact against slavery include Denmark Vesey, Sojourner Truth, Dred Scott, William Harvey Carney, Frederick Douglas, Sam Sharpe, Nat Turner, Olaudah Equiano, Ignatius Sancho, Booker T. Washington, Harriet Tubman, and Fredrick Douglas.

Slaves weren't allowed to vote during this time. Southern Representatives argued to have their slaves counted in the population. The delegates would be allowed to have more Representatives. The result was the dishonorable **"Three-Fifths Compromise,"** where slaves were counted as three-fifths of a free person.

Today, we are counted as one person. Everyone should vote regularly so your voice will be heard and the ballot can be counted when it's time to choose politicians, laws, and *amendments*. The *amendments* are changes to laws.

"I say from time to time that the vote is precious. It's almost sacred. It is the most powerful nonviolent tool or

instrument that we have in a democratic society. And we must use it."

John R. Lewis

During the final months of the Civil War, tens of thousands of freed slaves left their farms to follow General William T. Sherman's winning Union Army troops across Georgia and the Carolinas. After the Civil War, the first organized effort to give a type of reparations to newly freed slaves from 1863-1877 was known as **40 acres and a mule**. The black leaders first came up with this idea. Twenty black leaders had a meeting with the General William T. Sherman and Secretary of War Edwin M. Stanton in Savannah, Georgia. General William T. Sherman delivered Special Field Order Number 15, a short-term plan giving each freed family 40 acres of land. The federal government took away 400,00 acres of land from the Confederate landowners of the south. The 400 acres of land included a strip of coastline stretching from Charleston to the St. John's River in Florida, including Georgia's Sea Islands, and the mainland thirty miles in from the coast. The federal government failed to reorganize a majority of land back to most of the 3.9 million former slaves. Many African Americans still faced money-making hardships. The Union Army also gave some of its mules not needed for battle reasons to former slaves. The Northern armies moved through the South at the end of the war. Blacks began farming land left by whites.

Sharecropping was a labor that came out of the Civil War in the 1870s and continued until the 1950's. Landowners in the south still regularly required the labor of African Americans. *Sharecropping* and *tenant* (renter) *farming* was a major form in the South between the blacks and whites. **Sharecropping** was a system of farming in which the African American families rented small plots of land from the landowners. The African American families in return gave the landowners a part of their crops at the end of each year. Contracts between landowners and sharecroppers were normally tough and restrictive. Many contracts prevented sharecroppers from saving cotton seeds from their harvest making them increase their debt by getting seeds from the landowner. Landowners charged very high interest rates.

The years after Reconstruction, the South rebuilt many of the requirements of the black codes in the form of the **Jim Crow laws. Black codes** were restraining laws designed to limit the freedom of African Americans and guarantee their ease of use as a cheap labor force after slavery was ended during the Civil War. The Union victory had given some 4 million people in slavery their freedom. The question of freed blacks' status in the postwar South was still unresolved. Many states under the black codes forced Black people to sign yearly labor contracts; if they said, "no", they run the risk of being arrested, fined, and forced into unpaid labor. Anger over the black codes helped weaken the support for President Andrew Johnson and the Republican Party. These laws remained strongly in place for almost a hundred years. However, the laws were finally ended with the approval of the **Civil Rights Act of 1964.**

Roots was a well-known famous mini television series about slavery based on Alex Haley's 1976 novel **Roots**: The Saga of an American Family... A related film, Alex Haley's Queen is based on the life of Queen Jackson who was Alex Haley's paternal grandmother. The number of episodes were 8 but re-edited to 6 for video. The original release was from January 23 to January 30, 1977. The mini television series was first shown on the ABC network.

Grandmother Idella Green, Congressman John R. Lewis, Dr. Martin Luther King, Jr., Rosa Parks, James Mercer Langston Hughes, Jackie Robinson, Muhammad Ali, Maya Angelou, George Washington Carver, and other past influential black leaders with my African American roots also encouraged me to go to college. My grandmother had only a 3rd grade education but was a good reader and very smart with handling her daily activities. Grandmother said, "The children worked in the tobacco barns and fields to help provide money for their families. The children missed many days of attending school to work in the tobacco barns and fields." My father Bennie L. York, Jr., uncles, aunts, cousins, and other people also said, "They had experience of working in the tobacco barns and fields." Father said, "He would go home following school, take his school clothes off right after he got there, put on working clothes, and go to the tobacco barn or the field." Father also said, "He sometimes didn't go to school for 5 days in a row because of working so much in the tobacco barn or the field." The inability of our people not being able to gain knowledge and wisdom to get understanding made us to be left behind in learning *productive life skills* for generations to come.

After my high school graduation on June 7, 1988, it was time for me to get a job. I rode my bicycle on a Monday morning from my house to Winn-Dixie to look for a job. I walked into the store and went to the front counter of the office. The front counter was located a few feet straight ahead and slightly left of the entrance.

I asked the lady at the counter if there were any job openings. The lady went into the office and came back to the counter to tell me there were no job openings at this time. I went home and told my mother that Winn-Dixie didn't have any job openings. Mother told me to go and look at the schedule each day during the week like I was already working there, don't stop going to the store, and looking at the schedule until you get a job.

I went back to the store the next day and looked at the schedule. The schedule was on a clip board hanging on the side of the office towards the entrance of the store. I kept going back to the store for two weeks just to look at the schedule. Finally, one day when I was looking at the schedule, the Store Manager Mr. Miller looked down out of the office. Mr. Miller said, "I thought you were already working here because I saw you looking at the schedule almost every day." Mr. Miller told me to come back on Monday morning and be ready to work. I worked all summer as a grocery bagger and a shelf stocker. This was the same store manager who my grandmother Idella Green had told when I was a little boy, "This is a special child who is going to be great one day."

The night before going to Alabama State University which is located in Montgomery, Alabama, I packed up my clothes in three large toilet tissues boxes and three large paper towel boxes. I had taken the big boxes from the back storage room of Winn-Dixie. I also placed a small red Gideon bible under my clothes in the bottom of one of the boxes.

I was very excited on the drive to college with my parents during the Sunday morning. Father, mother, and I started getting hungry, so we stopped at Mr. J's Restaurant which was located just across the Florida and Alabama line. We went inside the restaurant, paid for the food, and walked to the buffet line. We sat down at the table at 10:30 am. A small amount of people was in the restaurant. Father and mother finished eating about 40 minutes after they had sat down to the table. However, I was still eating along with kept going back and forth to the buffet lines. The time was moving close to 4:30 pm. I had eaten a total of 36 chicken breasts, thighs, and leg quarters along with sliced turkey, ham, and meat loaf. I also had eaten rice, macaroni cheese, mash potatoes with gravy, fried okra, collard greens, and green beans. My deserts included cake, peach cobbler, apple pie, and ice cream. I had drunk several cups of sweet tea, lemonade, fruit punch, and soda.

My father and mother along with two of the restaurant's managers were watching me. The two restaurant's managers were sitting across the room from us. Father, mother, and I were getting up to leave the table when the two managers started laughing at me. Mother said to the managers, "My son is a football player." The managers had a receipt machine on the table in front of them as they were working on the business of the restaurant. Father looked at me and said, "Son you have eaten up the restaurant's *profit* for the month!" My parents started to laugh at me as we left the restaurant. We walked toward the front door to leave and the teenager girl cashier laughed at me.

My father and mother gave me goodbye hugs as we stood in front of George N. Card Hall on Sunday evening. I looked up in the sky and realized, I was in the real world. My dormitory named Benson Hall was located beside George N. Card Hall. I went into my room and took most of my clothes out of the boxes to place them in the dressers. I then placed the rest of the boxes with the clothes and the bible in the closet.

I laid down in the bed on the stomach with tears in my eyes, and the head towards the end of the bed at 7:30 pm on Friday night. My roommate Darrin stood across the room looking at me as I laid down on the bed. Next, I placed the little red Gideon bible on the floor below my head. Furthermore, I opened the bible to my favorite scripture to read it many times and started to cry. I had become very lonely being away from home in the new location. My favorite scripture reads; In this manner, therefore pray, Our Father in heaven, hallowed be Your name, your kingdom come, Your will be done, on earth as it is in heaven, give us this day our daily bread, and forgive us our debts, as we forgive our debtors, and do not lead us into temptation, but deliver us from the evil one, For Yours is the kingdom and the power and the glory forever, Amen (Matthew 6:9-13). I was reading, crying, and saying thank you, Jesus over and over again by the middle of the night. I woke up at 3:30 am in the morning with my head hung over the end of the bed and wet pages of an open bible on the floor directly under my head. I was very weak from crying most of the night into my bible. I felt refreshed and strong like the Lord had restored my strength.

Darrin's sister mailed him a big yellow envelope with items. The big yellow envelope included in it a cassette tape of the song "I Give All My Love to You" by Keith Sweat. Darrin played this song very frequently on his portable boombox radio cassette player for weeks when he was in the dormitory room.

The next week, the freshman students were given orientation on Tuesday. I went to the auditorium and sat down in my seat. The feelings of nervousness and excitement were among the young students. A few minutes later a man walked across the stage and said, "Welcome freshman class of 1988!" Some of the students stood up out of their seats clapping and then set back down. The man began to speak slowly and said, "Look to your right and then look to your left because one of the people sitting next to you will not be back to school next year. The facts state 50% of freshman students don't make it to their second year of college. The reasons are students may find out college is not for them because of their goals, poor grades, money problems trying to pay for school, become pregnant along with other issues. Students stay focus on the reasons why you are attending college!"

I was signing up for class in the gymnasium on Thursday in the same week. A lady was sitting second in the row of seven advisors for the signing up of classes. The advisors were selected to signed up classes for students by their last names. I had waited patiently in the registration line for the advisor. I didn't pass the ACT college entrance test, so the advisor was signing me up for all developmental classes for the first semester. The advisor said, "The developmental courses will not count towards your graduation but the hours for the classes will count as credits." Can I play football this year? The advisor said, "Don't worry about playing football this year and just focus on your grades!"

The next week on Tuesday, I went to the financial aid office to sign up for money to help me pay for my classes. I went to the office and saw two girls were already sitting in front of the financial aid officer. I sat in the third chair on the far-right of the row next to the two girls. The lady said, "You all are eligible for student grants, loans, and college work study. However, the college work study is a job, so you will be assigned to an area to work on campus." The financial aid officer asked, how will the three of you would like to have college work study in the cafeteria? First of all, the girl was sitting in the far-left chair said, "No." Secondly, the girl was sitting in the middle chair said, "No." Finally, I said, "yes, I'm not afraid of hard work and need to get bigger to play football." Because narrow is the gate and difficult is the way which leads to life, and there are few who find it (Matthew 7:14).

I had *regularly attended, studied smart* and *hard* with *good behavior* in my classes to have success during the semester. I got an A in four classes. I got a grade of B for the other two classes at the end of my first semester.

I was a hard worker in the cafeteria. A couple of staff workers and I cleaned the food from the dirty dishes, silverware, and trays as the students placed them in the window before we put them into the dish washer. Next, we took the dirty dishes which included plates, forks, spoons, knives, cups, and trays then put them into the hot steam water dish washer. We went to the other side of the long dish washer and took the items out. Some of the dishes and silverware needed to be sent from side to side of the dish washer again because they weren't clean enough. We dried many of the dishes with drying towels as they came out of the dish washer.

A small silver and black radio was sitting at the left side in the dishes return window. The radio played great songs during this time, but one of my favorite songs was "I'm Not Your Superwomen," by Karyn White. I really liked to listen to the song. The song gave me motivation as I was working in the cafeteria.

The women who worked in the cafeteria loved me because I was a good person and hard worker.

We cleaned off the tables in the dining room, swept and mopped the floors. One day during lunch, I was wiping off a table and removing the dirty dishes, silverware, and trays from it. Two of the players on the football team were sitting at a close by table and laughing at me. I thought to myself, "After I go out for the football team next year, no one will be laughing at me." During many occasions, the women allowed me to take food back to my room at the dormitory. Therefore, many times I gave my roommate food because I had so much.

I did a lot of preparing for the tryout with the football team during my first year in college by working out in the weight room, was running on the track field and the roads. My height was 6'1, weighed 205 pounds, and benched pressed the weight of 365 pounds at the end of the first year.

One day on a Friday afternoon, I was jogging on the track field at the Hornet Stadium by myself. Hornet Stadium is the on-campus practice facility for the football, track and field teams. I looked up to see my brother who drove from Quincy, Florida. He was just standing outside of the fence watching me run. I waved my hands to my brother, and he waved back to me. He came on the track field and watched the rest of my work out. Brother stayed the rest of the weekend with me on campus. Brother wanted to spend time with me and to get away from home for a while.

Since I had done very good with my grades the first semester, the academic advisor signed me up for four developmental courses and two real college courses at the beginning of the second part of the year which was my second semester. I got an A in five classes and only one B for the other class.

CHAPTER 5

THE PLAYING DAYS

I walked onto the football team at the beginning of August 1989, my first season with no scholarship during the start of the second year in college. I studied sometimes the assignments in my playbook between team meetings, weight lifting, and practices throughout the training camp. I took multivitamins during the camp to help me not to lose a lot of weight. I was just as good or better than most of the players who were on scholarship, but I was placed on the practice squad. The practice squad was known as the scout team.

Reginald Brown was a family friend and a fire fighter who gave my parents one pair of black and gray Newman gloves to give to me. Mother mailed the gloves to me.

I wasn't allowed to travel with the team even though I was a very good player. I was only allowed to dress out for the home games downtown at the Cramton Bowl.

I went home in May 1990 to spend time with my family and friends for the training of my second season. Many times, I went to the weight room at my old high school combined with the running in the afternoons. I walked or rode my bicycle from home to the weight room.

I was running from my home to the other side of town and then back home. I was jogging one afternoon about 3:30 pm on the sidewalk by the street in front of Winn-Dixie. A car with two men rode beside me. The man on the passenger side said, "You are going to die out there in the hot sun!" I looked over at the driver of the car then to the passenger and smiled at them as I kept running.

The football team was assigned to live in George N. Card Hall at the beginning of August 1990. The last Friday evening in August was almost the end of my second camp. I had studied the assignments in my playbook sometimes between team meetings, weight lifting, and practices throughout the training camp. I took multivitamins all the way through camp to help me not to lose a lot of weight. After each player was on one knee surrounding the head coach, the head coach said, "Don't make plans to go home for the three-day weekend. You will stay here and labor on Labor Day." I was just as good or better than most of the players who were on scholarship. However, I was placed once again on the scout team.

The fourth game of the second season, the defensive coordinator told me at the beginning of the week to practice with the first kickoff team because we are going to give you a chance to start on it this week. I called home and told my mother that I would be starting on the kickoff team on Saturday night which was a home game. I had practiced all week, so I was ready and excited to play on Saturday night. I was walking up and down along the sideline. I looked up in the stadium stands to smile and wave at my family and friends. The beginning of the game, I was about to run on the field to be on the kickoff team while the defensive coordinator was talking on his head phone set. Coach took hold of me by my left arm. Coach said on his head phone set to the other coaches, "He is not ready to play yet." Coach didn't allow me to play at all during the game. I was very hurt and disappointed that I didn't get a chance to play. My family and friends had drove from my hometown to see me play.

After the fourth game of the second season, my roommate Darrin also was a walk-on player with the football team introduced me to his older guy friend. He didn't attend the university but lived in the community. The older guy was a true fan of Jerry Lee Rice Sr. and tried to copy his life after him. Jerry was a great wide receiver for the San Francisco 49ers in the National Football League. He also played for the Oakland Raiders and Seattle Seahawks in the National Football League. Jerry is a member of **Phi Beta Sigma Fraternity, Inc**.

The older guy came up on campus and met us on the track field. We did drills on the grass and in the shot-put pit along with running on the track field. My roommate and I walked to the older guy's house to just hang out with him and lift weights. The older guy was a great friend and mentor to us. He also helped to improve our football skills and knowledge. My football skills had gotten incredibly better in practice.

During practice at the end of football season, my linebacker position coach told me, I want to play you so bad, but the defensive coordinator will not let me play you. I saw the defensive coordinator as he was about to enter into the locker room at the end of practice. I ran to catch up with the defensive coordinator. I got by the side of coach and looked down into his eyes while talking to him. I asked coach, why I'm not getting a chance to play? Coach said, "I have been hearing you hitting players at the other end of the field for two years, but you can't play for me." Why I can't play for you? I have given this football program my best since I've been here! Coach looked at me and said, "You are not one of our players." Coach, why I'm not one of your players? You are not on scholarship, so we are not putting money in you. You are also a crazy and too aggressive player to be on my defense. I was very hurt and disappointed from what the coach had told me. I put my head down with tears in my eyes as I walked into the locker room.

The beginning of the spring semester on January 1991, my new roommate Louis was from Birmingham, Alabama. My roommate regularly wore his football jerseys and cut off pants at the knees from high school. Louis had a brother who previously attended college. Louis said, "Brother would say to burn the midnight oil." Louis and I studied regularly for quizzes and tests until three or four o'clock in the morning in our dormitory room throughout the semester.

The players trained for spring football practice at the end of March 1991. We were on the track field, and two coaches organized relay races with each coach having two teams of four players. The coach of the defensive line chose the players for his two relay teams. I was the last one chosen by the defensive coordinator to be on his advanced relay team, so I could run against the starting tailback from the defensive line coach's advanced team. I got nervous running against the starting tailback. The players arrived from around the track field. The starting tailback got to take off first because his teammate came in first. I had soon left the starting line and taken about ten steps when I pulled my right hamstring. *The pain was very bad, but I hopped around the rest of the track field to the finish line.* My team finished the race in last place. The coaches should have stopped me from running since they saw I had hurt myself. My hamstring got healed in three and a half weeks. I was healthy just before spring practice.

I had great spring football practices following my second season. After the last practice on Friday afternoon, each player was on one knee surrounding the head coach. The head coach said, "The black and gold game will be the offense verses the defense. The winner eats steaks, and the loser eats hot dogs." I said to myself, "Tomorrow I will not be eating hot dogs."

The next day on Saturday, the spring game started at 1:30 pm. I started at outside linebacker on the weak side of the defense which wasn't the side where the tight end lined up on the offense. I was told to run straight and sack the quarterback as soon as the football was snapped to the quarterback. The strong side linebacker lined in front of the tight end would hit the tight end and then go into the flats during pass coverage.

The first play of the game, the tight end was lined up next to the outside shoulder of the right offensive tackle. The tight end departed from the right side of the offense. The tight end arrived and lined up on my side beside the left offensive tackle, so I ran to the left end of the defensive linemen. I was the weak outside linebacker. The strong side outside linebacker was in front of the tight end ran to the right end of the defensive linemen and lined up in front of the tight end. My position assignment was to rush the quarterback once the football was snapped because it was a passing play. However, I rushed in and couldn't sack the quarterback because he was very fast. The quarterback ran down the sideline about thirty yards before anyone could tackle him.

The defensive coordinator took me out of the game until the beginning of the third quarter. The coach placed me back into the game because the player he replaced me with wasn't getting the job done. I came into the game and dominated on defense. The game announcer in the press box continued to say after almost every defensive play, York is on the tackle. I had close to 20 tackles at the end of the game.

The defense won the game. After the game, the players took showers and got dressed to have dinner in the cafeteria. The offensive players were standing in line in front of the defensive players. The offensive players picked up their food and passed by the defensive players to sit down. I said to myself, "You all are eating those hot dogs today." My defensive teammates and I ate our steaks.

The following Monday afternoon at the defense team meeting the defensive coordinator said, "We have a great player in this room, and he is not ready to play at this time." The defensive coordinator was talking about me.

CHAPTER 6

NEVER GIVE UP ON YOUR DREAMS!

After the 1991 spring football practice, I decided to stay and attend summer school. The male students lived in the Dr. Martin L. King, Jr. Hall during the summer months. I went to classes and studied intensely throughout the summer. I also trained very hard for football during this time.

July was the month to sign up for financial aid for the next school year. I got the letter informing me my financial aid request had been processed. I knew time had come to go to the financial aid office. I went on a Wednesday morning to meet with a financial aid officer. I sat down in the chair as the financial aid officer pulled up my information on her computer. The lady looked at me with an unhappy look on her face and said, "You are eligible for four loans this year. This is the only financial aid that you can get this year." I said, "I really want to stay in school and play football. However, I will not be going to school and playing football if I got to sign up for four loans to pay for school. I'm working very hard in the classroom and on the football field to have to sign up for four loans." I was an out of state student. The out of state students' tuition fees for school were higher than the in-state students' tuition fees. The *economy* (wealth) was low and hard to get a job. I made my mind up to leave college and go back home.

I decided to go to the locker room on Saturday morning to turn in my football equipment before my parents came that afternoon to pick me up. I had put in a lot of time and effort with *memories* of playing football from the childhood playing days in my yard and all the way through the neighborhoods, little league, middle school, high school, and the college years so it was the right thing to do. The team had just started to practice as a result I could hear them on the field. I started to take my equipment out of my locker, and felt like I had lost my whole life. I sat back down in my locker. I cried for a long time before I turned in my equipment by placing it behind the counter. I was asking God to give me another chance to go to college. Afterwards, I walked out of the locker room.

I went back home to live with my family. My

brother was in the military, and the family was still living in the city in the yellow house with red brick. The community was known as Subdivision or Lake Skillet. The family had started to build a new two-story blue and white wood vinyl house with a fire place in the Robertsville Community. The Robertsville Community is about 15 minutes away from Quincy.

After I left school, the **hornets** football program continued to be successful. The next football season, the **hornets** won **the 1991 SWAC Championship, 1ˢᵗ Heritage Bowl Champions, and the National Black Champions** with a record of 11 wins, 0 losses and 1 tie.

I volunteered as the head junior varsity football coach at James A. Shanks High School from August to October 1991. Mother said in January, "It's time for you to get a job now." I drove downtown early on a Monday morning to park my car. I had walked the sidewalks for hours but couldn't get hired because of the low availability of jobs. Many companies weren't hiring during this time because of the low economy.

I walked up to the front door of the fish house at 1:30pm. I went into the fish house. The fish house was owned and operated by an old white man, his wife, and their son. I was hired to do fish prepping, cutting, and the inventory. I didn't handle the money transactions of the cash register so as soon as someone put in a fish order, I cleaned and cut up the fish to fill their order. I worked at the fish house Monday through Saturday from 7:30 am to 5 pm but sometimes worked past the leaving time.

The store owner drove down in the fish truck to the coast to purchase fish on Mondays and Wednesdays. Once the store owner came back from his trip, the men of the store unloaded the wood boxes of fish into the storage house located in the parking lot. The storage house was a few feet away from the fish house. I carried and used a cart to get the fish from the storage house to the fish house during the week.

I took between 45 to 65 boxes of fish for prepping and cleaning from the storage house on Wednesdays' afternoons to the fish house. We spent many hours prepping and cleaning fish in most of the boxes with 100 pounds of mullet fish all during the course of Wednesdays' afternoons. The owners' son said to me on a Wednesday shortly after 12 noon, **"One thing for sure is that time does not stop."** I was very tired after taking all of the fish from the cooler to the fish house and helping to prepare them for the weekend. People bought a lot of fish on Thursdays through Saturdays so we were very busy during those days. I didn't get off from work most of the time until 7:30 pm on many Thursdays through Saturdays evenings.

I was the inventory person, so I took the fish back to the fish cooler as needed during the day. I was very tired, wet, and smelling like fish at the end of the day as I took the fish outside to the cooler. Once I got into the cold cooler, it made me cold to my bones as I *shook* (trembled) from the coldness and the sweat being on me. I placed ice on the fish as the ice melted and rotated the fish by pulling the boxes with the older fish to the front of the cooler. One Saturday night about 8 pm, I was singing *"2 Legit 2 Quit"* because I was extremely tired at the time while I was finishing up in the cooler.

My sister was calling me Mr. Mullet because I smelled like fish. After work the next Saturday, I took my sister and Cedrick Love to the MC Hammer's *"2 Legit 2 Quit"* concert for my sister's birthday in April. My sister said, "The concert was a great birthday present."

The owners of the fish house sold it and were retiring from work. Therefore, I started my new job in May of stocking groceries at Winn-Dixie during the days and nights. A month later, I started to stock groceries at the IGA store during the days and nights. The IGA store was located directly across the street from Winn-Dixie. I was working at both jobs during the same time. I had done a great job at Winn-Dixie. The week after July 4th, I walked from back of the cash registrars' lanes towards the front office when Mr. Miller looked out from the top of it. Mr. Miller asked me if I wanted to be transferred to the produce department because they needed two more people. I said, "yes" because I knew the transfer to the produce section would give me some new and good work experience.

The middle of July, I was working in the produce department while spraying the vegetables by the front door. Coach Rodell Thomas walked in and stood beside me. Coach Thomas said, "You are a good person and athlete, so why are you back in Quincy?" I told Coach Thomas I didn't have enough money to stay in school, so I had to drop out and come back home. Coach Thomas said, "I'm taking Eric Hinson and Damon Sharp to visit Kentucky State University. I want you to go with us." I said, "yes" to the trip for going to the Bluegrass State.

Coach Thomas drove all the way with the other two players and I to Frankfort, Kentucky which is about a 12-hour trip from Quincy. We arrived late Friday afternoon and saw a lot of skunks running all over the campus especially in front of Kentucky Hall.

I thought to myself, "The only time when I had seen a skunk was on television." We went to the men's dormitory called Young Hall to take our clothes to our rooms. The dormitory was mainly used for upper classmen and students who participated in extracurricular activities such as football, basketball, baseball, band, golf, track and field etc. The dormitory was located near and across the road from campus. We went back on campus and walked around to see the skunks again. We smelled the skunks' terrible scents. Coach Thomas told us not to get to close to the skunks because if one of them spray you, you will need to take a bath in tomato sauce and it will take at least a week to get rid of the scent.

We had a good weekend visiting the campus, the football stadium, practice fields, and the locker rooms. Coach Thomas and I walked near the doors to leave the cafeteria Sunday afternoon when Coach Thomas asked me to attend the school. Coach Thomas said, "They need players and you will get a chance to play here."

Eric Hinson had played at Havana Northside High School and decided not to attend Kentucky State University, so only Damon and I were going back to attend the school. The week after Coach Thomas, Damon, and I arrived back home, Coach Thomas helped Damon and I to complete our financial aid paperwork at his house in the driveway just outside of the garage. Coach Thomas and his wife lived in a community known as Circle Drive.

The week before my trip, I went to the Allen Sports store. I bought two green wrist bands, two gold wrist bands, and a pair of green shoe strings. I was ready at this time to play football. The parents of Damon and himself arrived to pick me up from my house early on Saturday morning. Damon's mother and step father Roosevelt Brown who was the assistant coach of Damon's and my little league football team drove us to Kentucky State University. Damon had played football at the same high school a few years after me.

Before I went to football camp during the summer, I had great workouts at the gym with Jeffery "Jeff" March and Madison "Gee" Johnson from high school who were playing football at Tuskegee University. These were outstanding football players who were All-Americans and should someday be in the Hall of Fame. Madison and I had great workouts with Rodney Martin at his home. Rodney had attended the same high school and was a neighborhood friend.

CHAPTER 7

A CHANCE FOR GREATNESS

I had a great summer football camp in August of 1992. My height was still 6'1, weighed 211 pounds with a bench max press of 445 pounds at this time. I studied sometimes the assignments in my playbook between team meetings, weight lifting, and practices throughout the training camp. I took multivitamins during the camp to help me not to lose a lot of weight. The Defensive Coordinator Coach Samuel Smith and Offensive Line Coach Joseph "Joe" Poe designed a special position for me that was called Thorobred. I was a big, strong, and explosive strong safety with great speed and football knowledge. My experience from playing at Alabama State University helped me to learn and adapt quickly to the defensive plays during practice with making very few mistakes. The Kentucky State University's sports program wasn't in a conference during this time.

I placed a poster of Ronnie Mandel Lott on the wall beside my bed. Ronnie was a hard-hitting cornerback, free safety, and strong safety for the San Francisco 49ers and the Kansas City Chiefs in the National Football League.

A defensive tackle lineman named Lonnie from Mississippi wore a perm hair style and with an upper body built like a truck. The grease from the perm hair style leaked regularly on the face of Lonnie. The lineman had a height of 6'3, weighed 275 pounds, and a max bench press of 545 pounds. Lonnie said, "A small man like you should not be able to bench press that amount of weight. You must be down there in Pahokee, Florida wrestling those alligators!" Lonnie was sometimes in his dormitory room at 3 am in the morning and playing a song by the Ghetto Boys very loud on his portable boombox radio cassette player. He was screaming loudly at the same time.

I was named the starting strong safety by the Defensive Backs' Coach Mark Welch before the first game of the season. The game was a home against Findlay University from Findlay, Ohio. A huge crowd was in the stadium at 7:30 pm on Saturday night with the football excitement from the fans in the air. Alumni Stadium is located about a mile away from campus. After I got dressed in our locker room, I was still sitting in my locker. I started to think about the good memories of my grandmother Idella Green. I wrote the initials of I.G. with a black marker on the inside and outside of my white wrist tape on both wrists. I also had a thought about Jeffery "Jeff" March who was a great hard hitting strong safety at Tuskegee University. I was running from sideline to sideline the whole game making tackles on Findlay's running backs. The starting quarterback escaped free in the middle of our defensive line and linebackers for about a 15-yard run. I gave the quarterback a hard tackle in the middle of the field on our 40-yard line. I knocked out the quarterback with a hard hit in the middle of the third quarter, and he didn't come back into the game. I played a great game with the total of 16 solos tackles and 8 assisted tackles. The final score was Findlay University 14 and Kentucky State University 7.

The following Monday, I went to the weight room and worked out at Alumni Stadium. After the work out, I went to the coaches' offices and by the sports information director's office. The sports information director told me I'm going to notify the sports media in Quincy, Florida to tell them about the outstanding game that you had this past Saturday night.

After the third game of the season, Reginald Brown gave my parents a pair of white and gray Newman gloves to give to me. Mother mailed the gloves to me.

I went to the track field on Friday and Saturday nights to run the stairs for hours and in the soft sand of the long jump pit. I wouldn't go to most of the campus parties after the Saturday home games.

The sixth game of the season was against North Carolina Central University in Durham, North Carolina. I was told during the week our defense had to play against a big and fast tailback in which three NFL scouts would be at the game watching him. I also was told to turn the ball carrier inside on running plays to the two inside linebackers and the free safety.

The moment before kickoff, I looked across the field on a Saturday afternoon at 1:30 to the front goal post. I saw in the parking lot behind the goal post that our fan bus had not arrived for the game. I then looked up in the stadium stands and saw the three NFL scouts wearing the hats of the teams they were representing.

The first three series of offensive plays North Carolina Central University had possession of the football they scored three running touchdowns. I was taking on the big offensive linemen who blocked me at the left end of the offensive line. I forced the big and fast running back to run inside. However, the two linebackers and the free safety weren't getting over fast enough to tackle the ball carrier. The tailback had run for 229 yards and scored three long touchdowns along the sideline before the end of the second quarter. Our offense didn't score in the first half. The halftime score was Kentucky State University 0 and North Carolina Central University 22.

The beginning of halftime as our team was about to leave the field and walk to the locker room, I looked up across the field and saw the fan bus arriving to the stadium. I thought to myself, "I must do something to stop this running back." I made up my mind that I was going to lead our defense to stop the running back as I was stepping into the locker room. I would need to be more aggressive when the offensive lineman is trying to block me and go inside to make the tackle.

After halftime as I walked on the sideline, I looked up in the stands and saw our fans cheering for us. I got very excited and was ready to play. North Carolina Central University received the kickoff at the beginning of the second half so their offense had the football during the first series of offensive plays. The first play from the line of scrimmage as the running back ran the football straight to the middle of the defense when our big right defensive lineman tackle stood up the running back up trying to tackle him. I came across the top of the ball carrier with a hard hit to help *wrestle* him to the ground. The next play, the running back ran to the middle of the defense again but this time it was a big opening. I ran and tackled the running back with a hard hit. The hard hit stood the running back up and then I placed the running back on the ground. I was getting up from the ground, and I looked down at the running back. I said, "Get your big A** up!" A referee ran up behind me and said, "Number 43 if you say that again, I will kick you out of the game." I looked down at the referee into his eyes and nodded my head as I went into our huddle. Our offense came alive and started to score passing touchdowns up and down the field with some running plays. The offense scored 34 points by the end of the fourth quarter.

The offense of North Carolina Central University only scored one more touchdown in the third and fourth quarters. The running back only gained a total of 34 yards on the ground and didn't score a touchdown during the second half, so the offense tried to pass the football. The final score was Kentucky State University 34 and North Carolina Central University 29. Our fans were cheering and celebrating very loudly in the stands. I walked along the sideline in front of our fans with one of my right fingers in the air and my helmet in the left hand. I was saying we're number one to our fans. **Let's go Thorobreds!**

The last home game of the season was against Elizabeth City State University out of Elizabeth City, North Carolina. A week before the game, I was told by one of my teammates that our football team had went to Elizabeth City State University and beat them the year before when they were on their way to the playoffs. I knew this team would be coming to Frankfort, Kentucky with a chip on their shoulders, angry, and seeking revenge. One of my teammates was a defensive/corner back who transferred from Arkansas Pine Bluff told the defensive backs to be careful. The Vikings have a fast receiver who only ran fly and posts pass routes. The receiver also had transferred from Arkansas Pine Bluff. Coach

Samuel Smith told the defense during the week, the Vikings' offensive line averaged the height of 6'3 and the weight of 295 pounds. I knew it would be a fast, physical, tough, and *violent* game.

The game was on a Saturday afternoon at 1:30, our team was warming up at the far end zone of the football field. I was standing in front of the second goal post on the 40-yard line near the left sideline. The Vikings came jogging out of their dressing room onto the field in a single file line down the sideline. Twenty players ran onto the field. I thought to myself, "We must be playing today against the Dallas Cowboys." This team was very big with their uniforms being white with the numbers of the jerseys and their paints trimmed with the colors of blue and red.

The third play of the first series of plays a receiver ran a short post pattern from the left side of the field. We were in a cover two defense with deep two safeties on each hash mark. I was the strong safety and lined up on the right deep hash mark of the field. The receiver arrived in front of me in my zone and the pass was thrown to him. I tried to jump the play but misread how fast the receiver was and the placement of the football. The receiver caught the football beside me and ran down the sideline for a 40-yard touchdown.

I was walking off the field to go to our locker room at halftime. One of the defensive backs' coaches met me as I was coming off of the field. Coach David Boyd told me when the receiver run in your zone like that you must make the play. I had to play more careful while staying aggressive.

The first three series of plays at the beginning of the third quarter, the Vikings offense ran nine straight running plays. We were still playing the cover two defense with me now being on the deep left hash mark of the field. The two running backs lined up in an I formation with the tailback being directly behind the fullback and both of them weighing over 220 pounds. The running backs took turns running the football just outside of the offensive tackle and inside of the wide receiver down the hash mark. I was filling the alleys and tackling each running back between five to ten yards down the field. The running backs were extremely big and they were running very close to the ground. The only way I could tackle the running backs were to go lower than them and chopped their legs.

The first play of the fourth series of plays I ran up to the line of scrimmage. A big offensive tackle with the height of 6'6 and weighed 325 lbs. told me little buddy you better not keep running up here. The running back was tackled on the play already before I could get to him.

The fifth series of plays the Vikings started back passing the football. The tight end had the height of 6'5 and weighed 265 pounds was lined up on the left side of their offense. Our defense was still in the cover two defense, so I was the deep safety on the left hash mark of the field. The tight end ran a drag pattern across the field. I saw the tight end coming out the corner of my right eye as he arrived into my area. The tight end was running free behind the linebackers, and then the quarterback threw the football to tight end. I thought to myself, "This will be a knock out and a highlight film hit. The tight end will not get up from the ground for a while." I leaped into the air with both of my feet to hit the tight end in the middle of his chest but bounced off because he was very big. I came down on the ground face first. I turned my head to the side as I was still laying on the ground. I saw the tight end gave the football to the referee on the three-yard line. The tight end was standing straight up with the free safety laying on the ground face first holding onto the tight end's right ankle with both hands. A corner back also was laying on the ground face first holding onto the tight end's left ankle with both hands. The referee had blown the football dead because the two players stopped the tight end progress toward the goal line. I thought to myself, "Wow!" I gave the big tight end my best shot, and he was still standing up. I believe the Vikings scored on the next play.

The last series of plays the Vikings were passing and mostly running the football down the field. A running back on third down had run the football to our four-yard line. I tackled the running back chest to chest on the two-yard line, so he couldn't make it to the goal line. The part of the game was fourth down and only 53 seconds left on the clock. We got in our goal line defense, so I lined up on the right side of the defense in front of the tight end. The football was snapped and I stood the big tight end up on the line. Three of our players ran beside me in the backfield to make the tackle on the running back as the time went off the clock. The final score was Elizabeth City State University 40 and Kentucky State University 41. Our fans were very excited and celebrated in the stadium. I walked slowly off the football field and passed by the K-rettes as I was about to enter into the field house. The K-rettes were standing along the fence near our team's entrance into the field house. I stopped at the door before going into the field house. I turned around for a short time. I saw the fans still celebrating in the stands and walking out of the stadium. I turned back around and entered into the hallway to go to the locker room. **Let's go Thorobreds!**

The next morning, I rested in bed. My roommate Damon Sharp asked me are you going to the Sunday brunch at 10:30? I was hurting very bad with my bones aching from head to toe. I told my roommate; I couldn't make it to brunch and would try to go to dinner. I got out of my bed at 3 pm and left the dormitory at 5:30 pm.

Coach Smith had just left the field house which have inside of it the locker room and equipment rooms. The track field, practice field, and the field house were located across from the main side entrance road to the dormitory. The practice field was surrounded by the track field. The track field was made of broken pieces of hard asphalt rocks, dirt, and sand. The practice field was located in front of the field house. I had walked halfway from my dormitory towards the underground tunnel that guided everyone to campus. Coach Smith drove his car next to me and said, "You couldn't stop the hook pattern and then smiled at me." I gave Coach Smith a smile while shaking my head and started back walking towards the cafeteria.

After the game on Monday morning in biology class, the students were walking around in class while working on a science project. Tina Brown was one of the dancing K-rettes for the band. Tina said, "Eric your uniform was very dirty when you came off of the field."

After the game on Monday afternoon in Young Hall's lobby area, Linebackers' Coach Stokely Miller and I were passing each other. I was walking down the stairs to the lobby. Coach Miller was leaving the lobby and walking up the stairs to the rooms. Coach Miller said, "You were filling those alleys."

The last game of the season was against Jacksonville State University in Jackson, Alabama. Jacksonville State University is known as the Gamecocks. The week of preparation before the game, Coach Smith and Coach Welch told the defense to watch out for the cut blocks. The players on offense especially the offensive linemen chopped the legs of the opposing players on defense. You will play as the third inside linebacker this week. Most of the week during practice included drills in which the defensive players would put our hands towards the ground while staying in a low position to avoid blockers.

The game was on a Saturday at 1:30 pm at the Burgess-Snow Stadium. Our team was in the locker room getting dress before the game. I overheard the sports information director telling another player that I'm going to give you this number of tackles and York will get this number of tackles. This will give you the most valuable defensive player trophy for the year. I was very hurt from this because I had a great season and led the team in tackles. I stayed focused on my *assignments*. I didn't allow the conversation to distract my game preparation.

I was the first player of our team to go on the field for pregame warm ups followed by the other four starting defensive backs. I left the locker room jogging towards the goal post. I looked up in the stadium stands and saw the fans in the stands waving rebel flags. I looked down at the fans' red shirts and saw rebel flags on the front of them. I looked up in the sky as I was jogging behind the goal post and said to myself, "Lord what have you gotten this country boy from Quincy, Florida into." The other defensive backs and I continued to jog down the sideline to go behind the other goal post. I looked up in the stands behind the goal post. I saw a small amount of people was sitting in this section. I also saw only three black men sitting in the middle of the stands each holding a brown paper bag. One of the guys said, "Where are those dancing girls you all have called the K-rettes!" All of the three men started to laugh. One of the other men said, "You all are from Kentucky, and we are going to send you back to Kentucky with a butt whopping!" We jogged around to the other sideline and then entered the locker room.

The Game Cocks ran back the first kickoff for a touchdown at the beginning of the game. The Game Cocks continued to run back another kickoff and a punt for touchdowns before the end of the second quarter. Our defense was holding up good against the Game Cocks' offense. The Game Cocks were trying to run the football up the middle against our three inside linebackers. I didn't enjoy being one of the three inside linebackers this game because the offensive linemen kept trying to cut my legs.

We were in the dressing room during halftime. Coach Smith said, "I'm going to put the whole starting defense on the kickoff team at the beginning of the third quarter." The football was kicked off to the Game Cocks at the beginning of the third quarter. I was one of the two inside wedge busters who ran straight down the center of the field and no blocker touched me. I tackled the ball carrier on the four-yard line.

I had begun the third quarter as the third inside linebacker; however, the Game Cocks started to run options plays to the outside of our defense. I was placed at the right end of our defensive linemen. The other safety was moved to the left end of our defensive linemen. The other safety and I hit the quarterback so many times before he pitched the football to the tailback. The quarterback started to pitch the football and jumped back to avoid from being hit. The quarterback got rid of the football fast in the third and fourth quarters because of the pressure. The pressure helped the defense to react fast and make good plays. We were too far behind on the score board so it was a lost for us. Mostly small white children and some of them were black children holding autograph papers and pens at the end of the game. The children waited along the back of the fence. The fence was located behind our bench. Some of the players and I walked along the fence to sign autographs. The children were very excited as we signed their papers. We finished the season with a record of 4 wins and 7 loses.

I was very hurt from the conversation; I had heard in the locker room about the untruthful counting of the tackles before the game. I didn't go to the sports awards banquet after the season. I walked across the front of the student center on the side walk and dropped my head with small tears in my eyes before the start of the sports awards banquet. I kept walking past the student center. A small still voice whispered in the bottom part of my right ear said, "Vengeance is Mine." Beloved, do not avenge yourselves, but rather give place to wrath; for it is written, "Vengeance is Mine, I will repay," says the Lord (<u>Romans 12:13</u>).

The next week, I went to the football complex at Alumni Stadium to go to the weight room to work out. After I had finished working out, I went to the offices. Coach Smith gave me my K Club Letter because I didn't attend the sports banquet. The sports information director was no longer working for the University.

I played the first football season with no scholarship during the first semester of school. The only "financial student aid" I received was Pell Grants, Supplemental Grants, Federal Work-Study, and Student Loans.

I had arranged to ride with one of my teammates for the Christmas and New Year's holidays of December 1992 to his hometown of Montgomery, Alabama. After I arrived to Montgomery, Alabama, I planned to catch the bus home. My teammate and I were just about to put luggage into his car. My teammate said, "You can't ride home with me because my homeboy is riding home with me the same day." I was very hurt because two weeks before my teammate gave me permission to ride home with him. I caught a ride with another teammate who lived in Montgomery, Alabama and spent the night at his house. The next morning, my teammate took me to the Montgomery bus station. The bus ride gave me a feeling that I had accomplished something great the first semester of school, but a lonely ride home as I looked out of the window. Mother picked me up shortly after 2 pm in the afternoon from the Greyhound bus station.

After being home for about a week, I was watching television while sitting on the sofa. I turned the television to a channel and saw Findlay University was playing in the Division II championship game. I saw the starting quarterback who I had knocked out during our game against Findlay. The starting quarterback was playing in the game. The game was good and Findlay won by three points.

My father and mother bought my brother and I a car during my senior year in high school. After the Christmas and New Year's holidays, I was allowed with Damon to drive the car back to school. I had a sense that my college career was moving in the right direction.

I received financial assistance from the football

program at the beginning of the second semester of the year. The financial assistance continued in the course of my football career at Kentucky State University. The *atmosphere* was great with my educational and campus experiences, and the dormitory life. I kept good grades and trained hard during the winter and spring workouts. I drove back home with Damon to enjoy the summer vacation and to get ready for the upcoming football season.

I was visiting one day during the afternoon, one of the players who had played at the same high school at his house. The father of the player said to me, "You will not do as good as you did last year." I gave the father an unexpressive look on my face. I didn't respond to the comment.

My father, mother, and sister were temporary living in grandmother Alice Grace-York's trailer house while the new house was being built. The trailer house was located in the Greenshade Community which is about twenty minutes from Quincy. I trained very hard all during the summer for the 1993 football season. I went running from Monday through Saturday in the mornings and at 3 pm in the hot sun. I was running up and down the side of roads. I also was running up and down big hills along with going up them backwards which is called back paddling. I was in great shape but lost a large amount of weight.

Reginald Brown gave father a pair of white and gray Newman gloves to give to me. The gloves protected my hands from getting hurt and were especially good for the fingers. The gloves also helped to grip and catch the football better. I was very happy and thankful for all of the gloves because they were great gifts.

Ronald "Vicky" George lived about five minutes down the road from our trailer house. The Saturday evening before football camp, Vicky placed new brakes on brother and my car at his trailer house. I drove by myself at 12 o'clock the same Saturday night. I arrived on campus at 11:30 am Sunday morning for the August 1993 football camp.

I weighed in at 196 pounds for the beginning of camp. My body was trimmed down to mostly muscles. However, some of the coaches and players thought I was sick or something because of my weight loss. I studied the assignments in my playbook sometimes between team meetings, weight lifting, and practices throughout the training camp. I took multivitamins all the way through camp to help me not to lose a lot of weight. The school's sports program still wasn't in a conference during this time.

The defense struggled during three games in the season which caused the whole defense not to play at all in the three games after them. I still had a good season this year because I played hard whenever I got a chance to play. We finished the season with 2 wins and 9 loses.

CHAPTER 8

SPEAK TO THE MOUNTAINS

It is important to have faith in the Lord and be driven by the purpose of your goals in life. I didn't want to spend my whole life in Quincy, Florida without making something out of my life. I had decided at an early age to work hard and not be an average achiever. I chose not to participate with alcohol, drugs, cigarettes, and sex. I didn't want to get a girl pregnant and have a child before my high school graduation.

I have *love, character, integrity, respect, perseverance,* and *hope* which helped me to go through the up and down stages in my life. You should gain knowledge and wisdom from the seasons which produced the good and bad times, relationships with good and bad people, mistreatment to ourselves and others, mistakes by ourselves and others.

You should love yourself first, and you can't

make anyone love you. You cannot force a person's way of thinking to love and be truthful with you. The feelings you have for a person may be different from the way someone think of you.

Visionaries spend quality time being creative thinkers and working to manifest your *visions* and *dreams*. People may possibly try to distract and take you away from achieving the greatness of your goals. You must have a strategy and stay focus to *prioritize* (place in order) the importance of each goal for the achievement of success. You should use your *discernable spirits* to set apart the good people from the bad people.

You will block and destroy your own visions and dreams if you don't go after what you want out of life. Don't share your *visions* and *dreams* with everyone because you have *dream* blockers and destroyers. **Everyone will not support your *visions* and *dreams* as you walk in your purpose. Everyone will not support your purpose in life.** You must be very careful about telling people relating to the *things* in your personal life. The majority of people give attentiveness and truly be concerned about a few of people's conversations. You must be very careful when listening and following the advice from other people.

People may treat you wrong and do the same to other people. Everyone isn't for your good because they don't care about your health and if you become successful or not. Some people are only out to make themselves become successful and will knock you down to get it. Only a few people truly love and care about you.

The circle of people you have close relationships with should consist of *love, character, integrity, respect, trustworthy, perseverance,* and *hope* with their focus towards the achievement of positive goals.

It's a great reward if you have a least one true friend during your lifetime. Most people cannot give the names of at least five true friends. When people try to cause pain to you emotionally or physically, true friends do everything possible to make sure you are safe. They don't pay attention to who is trying to harm you; they will stand up for you at any time, and anywhere. If true friends can give assistance to you, they'll do it without hesitation or reward. A true friend doesn't constantly tell you about negative things other people say about you. First, true friends make it clear about the position they have when it comes to you by strong support with their words and actions. Secondly, true friends speak up for you when others are pulling you down with negative words and actions. True friends will help you and don't worry about the consequences. A true friend is a friend when it's a comfortable moment to give assistance and when it is not. A true friend will sacrifice to make sure that you're safe. A true friend regularly supports you when you are present and when you are not.

People who you put your trust in may not be honest with their expectations. People may not tell you the complete details about their expectations for your *performance evaluation*. You can be a good person, dependable, smart, and hard worker but still can't satisfy people.

Employers sometime give unmerited favor by the use of the **glass ceiling** to *employees*. The new employees, *associates* (friends, coworkers, colleagues), and family members with less education and job experience than the worthy employees may get the same position, better position or promotion. People don't always receive what they have earned and deserved with their education and experience. Employers aren't always fair with the use of *moral ethical standards* within the workplace.

But know this, that in the last days *perilous times* will come: For men will be lovers of themselves, lovers of money, boasters, proud, blasphemers, disobedient to parents, unthankful, unholy, unloving, unforgiving, slanders, without self-control, brutal, despisers of good, traitors, headstrong, haughty lovers of pleasure rather than lovers of God, having a form of godliness but denying its power. And from such people turn away! (2 Timothy 3:1-5)

So, Jesus said to them, "Because of your unbelief; for assuredly, I say to you, If you have faith as a mustard seed, you will say to this mountain, Move from here to there, and it will move; and nothing will be impossible for you. However, this kind does not go out except by **prayer and fasting**." (Matthew 17:20)

Stand therefore, "having girded your waist with truth, having put on the breastplate of righteousness, and having shod your feet with the preparation of the gospel of peace; above all, taking, the shield of faith with which you will be able to quench all the fiery darts of the wicked one" (Ephesians 6:14-16).

And whenever you stand praying, "if you have anything against anyone, forgive him, that your Father in heaven may also forgive your *trespasses* (sins, commit a fault). But "if you do not forgive, neither will your Father in heaven forgive your *trespasses*" (Mark 11:25-26).

The week before the end of the school year, I was in the cafeteria with four of my teammates in May of 1994. One of my teammates said, "I would get nervous if I get into a car accident." I said to my teammates, "I don't get nervous when I'm about to or get into a car accident." The following week on Friday, I went home. I got tired and sleepy sometimes while driving the 12-hour trip from Frankfort, Kentucky to Quincy, Florida.

I drove by myself back to school on August of 1994 at 12 o'clock on a Saturday night. I was on the interstate about three miles from the Kentucky line almost 9:30 am on Sunday morning. I saw an 18-wheeler truck that was a small distance ahead of me in the left lane. I was driving a little red Geo Prizm car in the right-hand lane. It was about 10 minutes later when a small still voice whispered in the bottom part of my right ear. The voice said, "Eric, the 18-wheeler truck is about to come over on you." Less than a minute later, I was at the right back side of the truck which was its blind side. The 18-wheeler truck came over into the right lane and forced me to go into the deep ditch. I didn't panic and could see nothing but tall pine trees. I went deep into the ditch but stayed calm and then drove the car out to the road with no scratch. The 18-wheeler truck was far gone up the road. If my car had gone into, went up or wrapped around one of those pine trees, I could have been out there for many hours by myself without anyone knowing about the accident. There were no gas stations and nothing but open road with the tall pine trees. **I came out of the pit!**

Once I got back to school, I kept lifting weights and training with our track team. I was very determined to get a football tryout. I searched the Canadian Football League's website in January of 1995 for the upcoming free agent try outs. I signed up and paid the registration fee to attend the camp of the Hamilton Tiger Cats in the middle of April of 1995.

I drove to Canton, Ohio by myself to attend the camp. After signing in at the registration table and getting my number, I stretched to get ready for the drills. The 40-yard dash was the first drill at the camp. I got down at the starting line and came up to run when the whistle was blown by the coach. After I ran about 10 steps, I pulled my right front thigh muscle which is called the quad muscle. I hoped the rest of the way to finish the 40-yard dash. I tried to run the second 40-yard dash as I hobbled terribly to the finish line. I participated with the rest of the defensive backs with drills during the three-day camp, but I was still limping extremely bad at this time. Most of the drills I participated in the head coach and two of assistant coaches were with him observing me performing the drills. The coaches followed me while I participated in the drills from station to station. The final day of the camp was completed after practice a line of players waited on the field to talk to the head coach. The head coach said, "The coaches really wanted to signed you for camp this month but we saw you had an injury. The coaches could tell that you were a real ball player." I said, "Thank you coach." I got in my car and drove back to Frankfort, Kentucky.

And not only that, but we also glory in *tribulations* (troubles, difficulties, sufferings), knowing that tribulation produces *perseverance* and *perseverance*, *character*, and *character*, *hope* (<u>Romans 5:3-4</u>).

"To realize the worth of the anchor, we need to feel the storm."

Brian Wood

"Life has a way of testing our anchors and tempting us to drift. Nevertheless, if our anchors are correctly placed in the rock of our redeemer, they will hold no matter the force of the wind, strength of the tide or height of the waves."

Brian Wood

"Three phrases of life are you going through something, about to go through something, you just got through something."

Brian Wood

One of my favorite songs is "My Soul Has Been **Anchored**," by Douglas Bell.

One of my favorite songs is "I believe I Can Fly," written and song by Robert S. Kelly, "R. Kelly".

But those who wait on the Lord, shall renew their strength; They shall *mount up* with wings like eagles, they shall run and not be weary, they shall walk and not faint (Isaiah 40:31).

One of my favorite songs is "I Don't Feel No Ways Tired," by Mighty Clouds of Joy.

One of my favorite songs is "Press My Way Through," The Williams Brothers presents Bishop Paul Norton by Lead Singer Bishop Neal Roberson.

One of my favorite songs is "Never Give Up," by Yolanda Adams.

One of my favorite songs is "My Testimony," by Marvin Sapp.

"An eagle soars above the clouds, never allow the storms and tribulations of life cause you to lose faith in your *visions* and *dreams*."

Eric S. York

We all experience pain in life, whether emotional or physical pain. No pain is alike, we must all walk the journey and path that God has for our lives, yet God promises that there is a purpose in all pain. We can press on each day knowing that our God loves us and wants to use the hurt and pain in this world to bring Him glory. (www.biblestudytools. com, Bible Verses About Pain

CHAPTER 9

JUST DO IT!

Always Put God First, Believe in Yourself, *Do Your Best*, **and Never Give Up on Yourself!** You must have a spiritual guide, have confidence in yourself, *give your greatest effort*, keep your determination, get help from the right people to give you strength and direct your steps during the up and down periods of life. You must not make *excuses* and *procrastinate* when accomplishing your *visions* and *dreams*. *Excuses* are tools of incompetence people who use them will never finish their purpose. *Procrastinate* is to wait or not take action towards the achievement of purpose. You cannot have *fear* at all times! You don't want to have memories of what could have happen which will give you *regrets in life*. You don't want to be one of the people who died that haven't started or completed their *purpose in life*.

"A lot of times we have fears of taking chances and stay in our comfort zones, we take our dreams to the graves."
Les Brown

Do your best before all the lights go off in your life. **I have sometimes looked back over my life.** Life is all about the seasons, we go through, and the ways we deal with them. My brother, sister, and I along with our neighborhood friends are all grown up now. Some of the neighborhood friends still live in the Subdivision/Lake Skillet Community; however, many of us have moved away. A few of the neighborhood friends have *deceased* (passed) away. We don't play activities with each other anymore. We talk by social media, telephone, or visit each other to have conversations about the good times. I can't play little league, middle school, high school, college football or run track anymore. A great high school football movie to watch is Friday Night Lights. The movie was released on October 8, 2004.

Write the *vision* down and make it plain on tablets that he may run who reads it (Habakkuk 2:2). It is important to have your *visions* and *dreams* written down so it can be visible for clear direction to the achievement of success. The *precise instruction* gives you the *character, focus,* and *structure* to become successful with your assignments. The use of *character, focus,* and *organization* leads to goals which are accomplished more effective and productive because of the knowledge and wisdom.

Are you clear on what your *personal values* and *priorities* are? I would suggest spending some time thinking and writing about what is most important to you in your life, and where you want to go with your life.

Once you have chosen what is most important to you in your life and where you want to go with your life, I would look at the ones you are trying to pursue. If they don't *balance* with your *values* and *priorities,* then I would consider dropping them, as they are not taking you to the ideal life you want to live. Generally, the goals that we don't want to put the effort and hard work into are those that don't line up with our main needs and beliefs. This exercise is a good system of removing the unnecessary from your life and getting you on track to living the life you want and need. (www.quora.com, Mark Military, Author of Practical Goal Setting. (www. Practicalgoalsetting.com)

For where your treasure is, there your
heart will be also

(Luke 12:34).

Do you want to be a Minister of the Word of God?
Do you want to become a school principal? Do you
want to become a school teacher? Do you want to
become a teacher paraprofessional? Do you want to
become a school counselor? Do you want to become
a college professor? Do you want to become a farmer?
Do you want to become an entrepreneur?

Do you want to be a computer professional? Do
you want to become a psychologist? Do you want
to become a scientist? Do you want to become an
airplane pilot? Do you want to become a politician?
Do you want to become a doctor? Do you want to
become a nurse? Do you want to become a lawyer?
Do you want to become a paralegal? Do you want
to become an engineer? Do you want to become
an architect? Do you want to become a carpenter?
Do you want to become a plumber? Do you want
to become an electrician? Do you want to be a
policeman? Do you want to become a fireman? Do
you want to become a news reporter? Do you want
to become a meteorologist? Do you want to become
a professional athlete? Do you want to become a

coach? Do you want to become an actor or actress? Do you want to become a salesperson? Do you want to become a store manager? Do you want to become an author? Do you want to become a motivational speaker? **Whatever you choose to do in life, *Just Do It!***

Actions speak louder than words! *Actions* **give productivity which measures the speed of output to the expected effort.** Once you have given your promise to participate in an activity, you should do your best to satisfy the commitment. If you can't fulfill the obligation, you should give a response. **Everyone doesn't keep their word. Everyone doesn't do, what they say, they are going to do.** You should do what you plan to complete with great *passion, humbleness, sincerity, concentration,* and *consistently* to have the excellence of production with your *assignments* (tasks).

> **"The excellence of quality is not what you do, but how great you do it."**
> **Eric S. York**

I have always believed that quality is more important than quantity when performing an action. It's not how long you live, but what you do with the life you live. But, let each one examines his own work, and then he will have rejoicing in himself alone, and not in another (Galatians 6:4).

I have accountability to God and myself to give my best ability every day by serving him, a good character, and do my tasks. I'm a person who serves God, give my best each day, treat people with respect, integrity, and fairness by good moral ethical standards. I treat people the way that I would like for them to treat me. I can look in the mirror during the day and before going to sleep at night with a good consciousness on my mind while laying my head on the pillow. I'm not a perfect person but living a righteous life in the eyes of God and to myself which is **personal accountability**.

I was inducted into **Phi Beta Sigma Fraternity, Inc.**, Xi Lambda Chapter, Muntu Dynasty on May 9, 1995 at Kentucky State University which is one of the greatest fraternities in the world. I have learned so much about life by being a member. I also have developed lifelong relationships and great memories with my brothers and the sisters of **Zeta Phi Beta Sorority, Inc.**

I was inducted into **Phi Theta Kappa Honor Society**, Beta Iota Omicron Chapter on May 22, 2002 at Keiser College in Tallahassee, Florida. Keiser College is known today as Keiser University.

I was honored with several academic honors which

included the Dean's Lists, National Dean's Lists, "Who's Who Among Students in American Colleges and Universities", The United States Achievement Academy", and the "National Collegiate Education Winner". I have a Master's Degree in Public Administration specializing in Human Resource Management on July 29, 2000, Bachelor's Degree in Physical Education Teaching on December 14, 1996, Associate's Degrees in Business Administration on September 27, 2002, and Accounting on November 19, 2004. I was featured throughout a National Collegiate Football Magazine during the 1992 football season.

I was honored as a Gadsden Author by the Gadsden County Democratic Women's Club at the Pat Thomas Law Enforcement Academy, Conference Center on May 31, 2019 in Havana, Florida. The Book Dedication of *Having Early Visions That Move Mountains, My Winning Purpose* to the Gadsden County Public Library was sponsored and hosted by the Gadsden County Democratic Women's Club on June 1, 2019 in Quincy, Florida.

I received a *vision* and *dream* from God at an early age which directed my steps of life with wisdom and understanding. The grace of God with determination helped me to overcome many trials and tribulations as I tried to pursue my purpose. After leaving the first college because of the shortage of money, I never gave up on graduating from college and becoming a professional football player. I walked onto Kentucky State University's football team with no scholarship and became one of the best players in history.

> **"Life is about your passion and drive."**
> **Les Brown**

> **"Greatness takes time."**
> **Bishop T.D. Jakes**

I was inducted into the Kentucky State University Athletic Hall of Fame on Friday, October 11, 2019. My wife Catina V. York, father Bennie L. York, Jr., and I went to my induction ceremony. The Hall of Fame Induction Ceremony was held at the Capital Plaza Hotel in downtown Frankfort, Kentucky. Father gave a two-minute introduction speech while I was walking to the stage. Father said, "Once Eric starts something, he completes it to the end." I was about to burst out crying but held it inside of me as I got near the stage. I thought about the days when father took brother Felix A. York, Sr., Joseph Washington III, and I to our little league games. I also remembered the many days of the children in the neighborhood playing sports with each other. I had good memories of my grandmothers Idella Green, Alice Grace-York, Marjorie Robinson, aunt Dorothy A. Hamilton-Reese, grandfather Bennie L. York, Sr., father Bennie L. York, Jr., mother Jacqueline V. York, brother Felix A. York, Sr., sister Jocelin L. York and her son Cameron York, wife Catina V. York, and Coach Rodell Thomas along with other family members and friends. Lastly, I had a reflection about all of the ups and downs during my life that I went through from playing little league sports to playing college football and the tryout with the Hamilton Tiger Cats. Once I got to the stage and started to give my acceptance speech, I was still crying inside of me and held it in for the first three minutes of my emotional ten minutes speech. ***Dreams Do Come True!* Glory Be to God!**

Coach Smith and I have kept in touch with each other throughout the years. Coach Smith told me during one of our telephone conversations that out of his 34 plus years of coaching, I was in the top three of the best players that he has ever coached.

It is important to have *peace, joy,* and *fulfillment* in life. You must find time to do those things which bring calmness, happiness, agreement, and completion in your lives. **You should enjoy life today because time does not wait, and tomorrow is not promise to no man.**

To everything there is a season, a time for every purpose under heaven; a time to be born, and a time to die; a time to plant, and a time to pluck what is planted; a time to kill, and a time to heal; a time to break down, and a time to build up, a time to weep, and a time to laugh; a time to mourn, and a time to dance; a time to cast away stones, and a time to gather stones; a time to embrace, and a time refrain from embracing; a time to gain, and a time lose; a time to keep, and a time to throw away; a time to tear, and a time to sew; a time to keep silence, and a time to speak, a time to love, and a time to hate; a time of war, and a time of peace (<u>Ecclesiastes 3:1-8</u>).

One of my favorite songs is "God's Grace," by Rev. Luther Barnes.

My favorite song is "Down Through the Years," by Jasper Williams Jr.

The race is not to the swift, nor the battle to the strong, nor bread to the wise, nor riches to men of understanding, nor favor to men of skill; but time and chance happen to them all (<u>Ecclesiastes 9:11</u>).

"Let's strive to achieve greatness, life is very precious and short."

Eric S. York

"How much time you have left to do, what you want to do?"

Les Brown

CHAPTER 10

THE BURNING BUSH

The story of God speaking to Moses out of the burning bush is found in Exodus 3:1—4:23. Through this remarkable event, Moses encounters God on Mount Horeb, and God reveals Himself (Deuteronomy 33:16; Mark 12:26). The burning bush as described in Exodus 3:2 is a theophany, the appearance of God in a form that is visible to man. The bush itself was most likely some kind of bramble or thorn bush, and the fire burning the bush was in the form of the angel of the Lord who "appeared to him [Moses] in flames of fire" (Exodus 3:2).

This is the first time the Bible uses the word "holy" with reference to God (verse 5). At the burning bush God revealed His holiness in a way it had never been revealed before. Moses was so awed by this experience that later when he wrote his famous victory hymn, he made sure to mention this divine attribute of God's holiness. "Who among the gods is like you, O LORD? Who is like you—majestic in holiness, awesome in glory, working wonders?" (Exodus 15:11)

There are several reasons why God revealed Himself to Moses out of the burning bush. First, God reveals Himself as a fire in that it is an image of His holiness. All through the Bible, fire is used as a picture of the purifying and refining quality of God's holiness. This is further evidenced when God commands Moses to remove his sandals "for the place where you are standing is holy ground." Here God was emphasizing to Moses the gap between the divine and the human. God is transcendent in His holiness, so Moses was not allowed to come close to Him.

Holiness involves separation. God's holiness means that He is set apart from everything He has made. Holiness is not simply His righteousness (although that is part of it), but also His Otherness. It is the distinction between the Creator and the creature, the infinite distance between God's deity and our humanity. God says, "I am God, and not man—the Holy One among you" (Hosea 11:9). His people respond by saying, "There is no one holy like the LORD" (1 Samuel 2:2).

Second, God revealed Himself to Moses out of the

burning bush as an image of His glory. Though this theophany was frightening (Exodus 3:6; Deuteronomy 4:24), its purpose was to manifest the sheer majesty of God and to stand as a visible reminder to Moses and his people during the dark times ahead. For it would be soon that God would manifest His holiness and glory to the entire nation of Israel. As Moses and the children of Israel soon learned, His glory is like a consuming fire, a pillar of fire that radiates light, a light so brilliant that no man can approach it (Exodus 24:17; 1 Timothy 6:16).

Then we see that God was also concerned for the suffering of His people Israel (Exodus 3:7-8). In fact, this was the first time God had ever called Israel "my people." Under the oppressive bondage of Egypt, they had no hope but God, and they could do nothing but cry out to Him. God heard them and was now going to meet their need by delivering them from their enslavement and suffering (Psalm 40:17; Isaiah 41:10; Jeremiah 1:8). Though God has revealed Himself as one who lives in unapproachable light (1 Timothy 6:16), the burning bush symbolized His intent not to consume or destroy His people, but to be their savior, to lead them out of bondage in Egypt and into the Promised Land.

Additionally, God gave Moses His own personal

name: "God said to Moses, 'I AM WHO I AM. This is what you are to say to the Israelites: "I AM has sent me to you" (Exodus 3:14). There are several reasons why God did this. The Egyptians had many gods by many different names. Moses wanted to know God's name so the Hebrew people would know exactly who had sent him to them. God called Himself I AM, a name which describes His eternal power and unchangeable character. "I AM THAT I AM," declares God to be self-existent, without beginning, without end. This is also expressed in the term *"Yahweh,"* meaning "I Am the One Who Is." It is the most significant name for God in the Old Testament.

By identifying Himself as "I AM," God is declaring that He always exists in the immediate now. He isn't bound by time like we are. There was never a time when God wasn't. He has no fixed point when He was born or brought into being. He has no beginning or end. He is the Alpha and the Omega, the First and the Last (Revelation 22:13).

Today, the only way for us to come into the presence of a holy God is to become holy ourselves. This is why God sent Jesus to be our Savior. He is our holiness (1 Corinthians 1:30). We could never keep God's Law, but Jesus kept it for us with perfect holiness. When Jesus died on the cross, He took away all of our unholiness, exchanging His righteousness for our unrighteousness (2 Corinthians 5:21). When we believe in Him, God accepts us as holy—as holy as Jesus Himself:

The *grace* that God has shown through the cross enables us to approach the Holy One—not as Moses did, hiding his face in fear, but by faith, trusting and believing in the person and work of Jesus Christ. (www.gotquestions?.org, "Why did Moses speak to God out of the burning bush?")

In Numbers 20:8, the Lord told Moses, "Take the staff, and you and your brother Aaron gather the assembly together. Speak to that rock before their eyes and it will pour out its water. You will bring water out of the rock for the community so they and their livestock can drink." Numbers 20:9-11 records Moses' response: "So Moses took the staff from the LORD's presence, just as He commanded him. He and Aaron gathered the assembly together in front of the rock and Moses said to them, 'Listen, you rebels, must we bring you water out of this rock?' Then Moses raised his arm and struck the rock twice with his staff. Water gushed out, and the community and their livestock drank." The Lord was displeased with Moses' actions: "Because you did not trust in me enough to honor me as holy in the sight of the

Israelites, you will not bring this community into the land I give them" (Numbers 20:12).

What did Moses do that warranted such a severe penalty from the Lord? First, Moses disobeyed a direct command from God. God had commanded Moses to speak to the rock. Instead, Moses struck the rock with his staff. Second, Moses took the credit for bringing forth the water. Notice how in verse 10 Moses says, "Must we [referring to Moses and Aaron] bring you water out of this rock?" Moses took credit for the miracle himself, instead of attributing it to God. Third, Moses committed this sin in front of all the Israelites. Such a public example of direct disobedience could not go unpunished. Fourth, it seems that God had intended to present a type of Christ in this circumstance. The water-giving rock is used as a symbol of Christ in 1 Corinthians 10:4. The rock was struck once in Exodus 17:6, just like Christ was crucified once (Hebrews 7:27). Moses' speaking to the rock in Numbers 20 was to be a picture of prayer; instead, Moses angrily struck the rock, in effect, crucifying Christ again. **His punishment for disobedience, pride, and the misrepresentation of Christ's sacrifice was that he was barred from entering the Promised Land** (Numbers 20:12).

(www.gotquestions?.org, "Why was Moses not allowed to enter the Promise Land?")

Moses was leading the children of Israel out of bondage to the land of milk and honey while God was guiding and assisting Moses with his purpose. Moses was a chosen vessel by God because of his humbleness and obedience. Moses became disobedient with sinful actions which caused him not to complete his purpose for the goal of leading God's chosen people to the Promise Land. God tries to speak to our minds and hearts in different ways, so we can be contacted to hear and accept by faith the knowledge and wisdom from God's voice. We must stand as a good solider for Christ during the hardships of life with the trials and tribulations to stay focus on our purpose.

CHAPTER 11

IMPACT LIVES

I was thirty-nine years old in Tallahassee, Florida when God whispered in the lower part of my right ear in a small still voice. "Eric, it is time for you to do something for me. It is time for you to impact men to help themselves with their personal growth, leadership of families, and communities." **I looked back over my life.** I knew the time had come for me to do something for the Lord. So, and He said to me, "Son of man, can these bones live?" So, I answered, "O Lord God, you know." Again, He said to me, "Prophesy to these bones, and say to them, O dry bones hear the word of the Lord! Thus, says the Lord God to these bones: "Surely, I will cause breath to enter into you, and you shall live." (Ezekiel 37:2-5).

God was letting me know that he knew me, and now is the time for you to walk in your purpose to influence and strengthen future generations to come. But the very hairs of your head are all numbered (<u>Matthew 10:30</u>). In all things showing yourself to be a pattern of good works; in doctrine showing *integrity, reverence* (respect), *incorruptibility* (no guilt, blamelessness), *sound speech* that cannot be condemned, that one who is an opponent may be ashamed, having nothing evil to say to you (<u>Titus 2:7-8</u>).

I wasn't afraid to not be successful when I hosted and spoke at the men conferences. I had started **praying and fasting** more for the conferences. I had to protect myself and other people against spiritual attacks.

The Men Leading Generations Conference and theme *"Men Get on Fire for the Lord!"* was brought to fulfillment in 2009, to encourage men to be more effective leaders through fellowship, teach principles of responsibilities to the home, church, and community. We must train ourselves through gaining knowledge and wisdom to successfully get men to come to Christ. *And He Himself gave some to be apostles, some prophets, some evangelists, and some pastors, and teachers, for the equipping of the saints for the work of ministry, for the edifying of the body of Christ, till we all come to the unity of the faith and of the knowledge of the Son of God, to a perfect man,* *to the measure of the stature of the fullness of Christ: that we should no longer be children, tossed to and fro and carried about with every wind of doctrine, by the trickery of men, in the cunning craftiness of deceitful plotting, but, speaking the truth in love, may grow up in all things into Him who is the head-Christ- from whom the whole body, joined and knit together by what every joint supply, according to the effective working by which every part does its share, causes growth of the body for the edifying of itself in love* (Ephesians 4:11-16).

I wasn't afraid to not be successful when I hosted and spoke at the youth conference. I **prayed and fasted** for the youth conference. I had to protect myself and other people against spiritual attacks.

The Youth Leading Generations Conference and theme *"Youth on Fire for the Lord!"* **"Stop the Violence"** was brought to fulfillment in 2013, to encourage children to be more effective leaders through fellowship, teach principles of responsibilities in the home, church, and community. Children must be taught and encouraged to live by the Word of God. **Spending quality time with children** is the most important gift that we can give to future generations. Children needs great role models so they can pattern their lives after successful people. The younger generation would have *maturity* (experience, wisdom) as they become adults by making better choices and decisions.

> **"The treasure of the heart is love which impact your passion to care for people, faith and love with a purpose give you belief, character, and perseverance to motivate the development of generations on the road to greatness."**
> **Eric S. York**

I know your works. See, I have set before you an open door, and no one can shut it; for you have a little strength, have kept My word, and have not denied My name (<u>Revelation 3:8</u>).

It's important for my purpose in life to support and pass down life lessons along with experiences to parents and the future generations. I have mentored, counseled, tutored children and young adults for years with their education and making good life choices. I have helped young people by being a minister of the gospel, a teacher, coached sports, getting them prepared and accepted into colleges, and the military. It's great to see the influence that I have made in young people lives as they become professional adults to positively impact communities.

I believe in motivating people and myself beyond our **comfort zones** in order to achieve success.

> **"Don't wait until everything is perfect to achieve your dreams, you must have faith."**
>
> **Les Brown**

> **"Life doesn't always go your way; however, keep the faith, take life one day at a time, stay respectful, take chances, hard work, and don't give up on the road to greatness."**
>
> **Eric S. York**

> **"Expect to win the race of life with your faith, humbleness, purpose, and hard work."**
>
> **Eric S. York**

Let's Get and Stay on Fire for the Lord!
In the Name of Jesus!
Blessings!

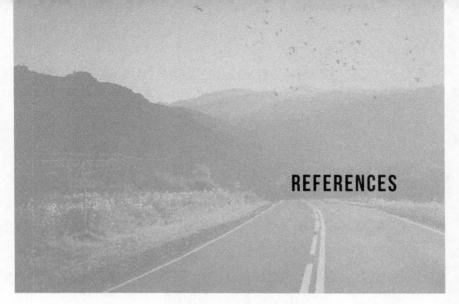

REFERENCES

1. www.ucg.org/the-good-news/gods-vision-for-you, Beyond Today, "Help for Today, Hope for Tomorrow" God's *Vision* for You! by Dale Schurter
2. www.abolition.e2bn.org/slave_40.html, The Abolition Project, What is Slavery?
3. www.nytimes.com/mag, 1619, When did slavery started in Africa?
4. www.history.com/first-a, Who was the first American Slaves arrived in Jamestown?
5. www.voanews.com/usa, Slaves sold for $1,200
6. www.The Varieties of Slave Labor, Freedom's Story, TeacherServe®, National Humanities Center, Freedom's Story, "The Varieties of Slave Labor" by Daniel C. Littlefield
7. www.digitalhistory.uh.edu, Slave Labor, "Digital History, Using New Technologies to Enhance Teaching and Research"

8. www.christianitytoday.com/history/issuses/ issue-33/secret-religion-of- slaves.html, The Secret Religion of the Slaves, They often risked flogging to worship God. By Albert J. Raboieau, CT Christian Today

9. www.history.house.gov/Institution, Proportional Representation/ US House of Representatives

10. www.pbs.org./wnet/africa-american-many-rivers-to-cross/history/the-truth- behind-40-acres-and-a-mule/ "100 Amazing Facts About Negro" The Truth Behind '40 Acres and a Mule by Henry Louis, Jr./ Originally poster on The Root

11. www.en.m.wikipedia.org/wikipedia, Sharecropping Wikipedia

12. www.64parish.org/entry, Sharecropping

13. www.britannica.com, Sharecropping/Definition, Description, History & Fact

14. www.history.com, Forty Acres and a Mule, Updated: Jun. 7, 2019, Original

15. www.history.com, Black Codes, Updated: Jan. 21, 2021, Original: Jun. 1, 2010, History.com Editors

16. www.biographyonline.net, Biography Online, Famous Slaves

17. www.en.m.wikipedia.org/wiki, The Movie Roots

18. Friendship Dynamics | What Is the Real Definition of a True Friend? | BetterHelp, What is the Real Definition of a True Friend? By Joanna Smykowski

19. www.biblestudytools.com, Bible Verses About Pain

20. www.quora.com, Mark Milotay, Author of Practical Goal Setting. www.Practicalgoalsetting.com

21. www.gotquestions?.org, Why did God speak to Moses out of the burning bush? Why was Moses not allowed to enter the Promise Land?

22. The Holy Bible, New King James Version, Copyright 1994 by Thomas Nelson, Inc.

ABOUT THE AUTHOR

Eric S. York received several academic honors which included the Dean's Lists, National Dean's Lists, "Who's Who Among Students in American Colleges and Universities", The United States Achievement Academy", and the "National Collegiate Education Winner". He has a Master's Degree in Public Administration specializing in Human Resource Management, Bachelor's Degree in Physical Education Teaching, Associates Degrees in Business Administration and Accounting. He was featured throughout a National Collegiate Football Magazine. Eric was inducted into the Kentucky State University Athletic Hall of Fame.

"**In Loving Memory of** Grandmothers Idella Green, Alice Grace-York, Marjorie Robinson, Grandfather Bennie L. York, Sr., Aunt Dorothy A. Hamilton-Reese, Uncle Curtis "Walking Curtis" Grace-York, Uncle Wesley Zackery, Sr., Father & Law Jeffery "Jeff" Robinson, Evangelist Ruthie Robinson Wester, Aunt Annette York, Aunt Doris Cox, Cousin Darrin "Big D" Jackson, Bernard Powell, Jr., Che Wayne Kincy, Rodney Martin, Ty Corker, Buster Smart, Gary Benton, Michael Tribute, Sr.-"Supervisor Jackson Heights, Quincy Recreation Department", Coach Bobby Nealy-"Southern Electric", Carolyn L. Bridges-Smith-"Speech Pathologist, Stewart Street Elementary, Zeta Phi Beta Sorority, Inc.", Reverend Nehemiah Bowers-"Pastor & Agriculture Teacher", Carl L. Daniels-"History & Social Studies Teacher", Coach James W. Pelham-"History Teacher, Track & Field Coach", Coach Charleston Lee Holt-"Principal, Teacher & Coach", Elder William M. Maxwell, Sr.-"Pastor of Mount Hosea Missionary Baptist Church", James Britton-"Housing Director of Young Hall, Kentucky State University", Coach Joseph "Joe" Poe-"Offensive Line Coach at Kentucky State University", Ronald "Vicky" George, Bobby Parker, Jr., Apostle Anthony "Tony" Sanders, Granderson "Dog" Johnson, Deputy Sheriff Brian Faison, Deacon Alto

Anderson, Deacon Arzell Diggs, Jr., Elder Lynfahia Arnett "Faye" Hills, Robert "Scotty" Jones-"KSU Phi Beta Sigma Fraternity, Inc.", Michael Jenkins-"KSU Phi Beta Sigma Fraternity, Inc.", Eugene "Jerry" Grice-"Ultimate Cuts Barber", Congressman John R. Lewis-"American Politician, U.S. Representative, Statesman, Civil Rights Activist, Phi Beta Sigma Fraternity, Inc.", George Washington Carver-"Famous Inventor, Phi Beta Sigma Fraternity, Inc.", *The Victims of the Coronavirus*

"**A Special Thanks to** My Wife Catina V. York, Father Bennie L. York, Jr., Mother Jacqueline V. York, Brother Felix A. York, Sr., Sister Jocelin L. York, Uncle Archie & Aunt Mary York-Jackson, Uncle & Pastor Eddie & Aunt Linda York, Cousin Sharon Richardson, Uncle Charlie York, Cousins Ray & Linda Walker, Charles Robinson, Joseph Washington III, Arness "Candy Man" Rittman, Errick Walters, Derrick Walters, Derrick Robinson, Jerry Vickers, Sister & Law Gloria Robinson, Sister & Law Ruthie Robinson, Mother & Law Catherine Robinson, Uncle George Cox, Reginald Colston, Alison Williams, Reginald Brown, Madison "Gee" Johnson, Cynthia Davis, Brenda Perry, Reginald & Betty James, Coach Rodell Thomas, Coach Charles "Chicken" Green, Coach Andy Gay, Coach Joe Ferolito, Coach Alexander James, Coach Brian Wood, Coach Mark Liles, Coach Isaac & Lori Livingston, Eric Hinson, Gadsden County Democratic Women's Club, Stephan D. & Natalie Turner, Jerel Coats, Daryl Coats, Terrill Easterling, Alexia J. Ellis, Dr. Troy Rawlins, Reverend Timothy & Felicia Taylor, Isadore Rich, Ron Banks, Valerie Shavers, Leslie Thomas, Coach Oscar Downs, Coach Maurice "Mo" Hunt, Dr. & Coach Vaughn Little, Coach Mark Welch, Coach Samuel Smith, Dr. & Coach Corey Hicks, KSU President Christopher

M. Brown II, Randolph A. Williams "Randy"-K-Club President, All of the Kentucky State University's K-Club Members & Supporters, All of My Past School Officials and Coaches, All of My Family & Friends, Subdivision/Lake Skillet Community"

"Thanks for the encouragement to write this book! Catina V. York, Felix A. York, Sr., David Slaton, Esq., Antonio Wright, Joseph Washington III, Arness "Candy Man" Rittman, Subdivision/Lake Skillet Community

Contact Information:
Email: impactyork@yahoo.com
Linktree: linktr.ee/impactyork6

CPSIA information can be obtained
at www.ICGtesting.com
Printed in the USA
BVHW031830010223
657618BV00002B/273